Supporting Children

with

Post-Traumatic Stress Disorder

A practical guide
for teachers and professionals

David Kinchin and **Erica Brown**

David Fulton Publishers
London

David Fulton Publishers Ltd
2 Park Square, Milton Park, Abingdon, Oxon, OX14 4RN

www.fultonpublishers.co.uk

First published in Great Britain by David Fulton Publishers 2001
Reprinted 2003

Transferred to Digital Printing 2007

British Library Cataloguing in Publication Data
A catalogue record for this book is available from the British Library.

ISBN 1–85346–727–8

Typeset by FiSH Books, London

Publisher's Note
The publisher has gone to great lengths to ensure the quality of this reprint
but points out that some imperfections in the originalmay be apparent

Contents

Dedication

With warm affection and gratitude, the authors dedicate this book to their spouses and parents. To Elaine and Alan our spouses, to Ann and Miles and Eric and Iris our parents, you have taught us through your example that strength and resilience is born out of adversity. For these gifts and your unconditional love, we give you our heartfelt thanks.

Introduction

David's story

Friday 31 July 1987 was probably the worst day of my police career (although I did attend a rather significant shooting incident in Hungerford three weeks later). On that Friday at the end of July I was sent to deal with a road accident in a quiet Oxfordshire village.

While playing in a peaceful residential street two children were totally absorbed in their game and blissfully unaware of the street cleaning vehicle as it went about the business of cleaning the gutters at the side of the road. The driver reversed into the two children crushing them (Kinchin 1988). Taya, eight years of age, and her cousin Thomas, thirteen, died instantly.

Pondering how I was going to identify the two unfortunate playmates I was aware of a teenage girl approaching the accident scene. She suddenly rushed forwards and knelt beside the blanket which had been diplomatically placed over the young bodies. Her movements were so quick that nobody reacted swiftly enough to stop her lifting a corner of the blanket. By the time she had been taken away from the scene she had inadvertently identified her brother and her cousin. Everyone was deeply distressed by the accident and the trauma was compounded by the actions of the young girl.

Approximately six months later I revisited the family and spoke at length with the girl's father. He still grieved for his son and niece. He also explained that his wife and daughter could not bring themselves to talk to me because of my part in dealing with the accident. His daughter had developed a phobia of policemen. As a family they remained deeply distressed by flashbacks and nightmares. The accident continued to occupy their thoughts for much of the day of my visit, even six months after the original accident. I did not have the courage to admit to them that the accident had also affected me in much the same way.

It is only confirmed sentimentalists who believe childhood is a time of uninterrupted joy and fulfilment. In our experience children often suffer distress in a world where traumatic events including bereavement, chronic illness, abuse and disasters are everyday occurrences.

Separately we have worked in different contexts and we acknowledge we both have our own theoretical bias and practical preferences – David as a teacher and police officer and Erica as a teacher and manager in schools and Higher Education and a senior manager in children's hospices. This book has emerged from our shared interest in the effects of loss and grief in children's lives. At the heart of the text is the philosophy that we owe it to the children to help them face trauma and in doing so to empower them to face the impact of their experience.

The aim of the book is to contribute to an improved understanding of the challenges and tasks that face children who are coping with trauma, and to guide the adults who care for them. In the course of writing we have drawn on the ideas, advice and memories of many people from different backgrounds, cultures and professions and we are indebted to them for their support and guidance.

It can be extraordinarily hard for children to embark on the process of acknowledging the impact of a traumatic event in their lives. It takes courage and determination to reflect on what has happened and to begin a journey full of grief and painful memories. The right of children to have their views heard is of prime importance. This right extends to telling their stories and it is our shared belief that studies do not adequately and accurately reflect the reality of children's experiences and responses unless their own accounts are taken into consideration.

People's attitudes towards trauma are in many ways dependent on the amount of experience they have of living or working with those who have experienced and survived traumatic events. Some professional carers may find it difficult to comprehend the loss of self-esteem which bereft children experience, and they may also underestimate the emotional wear and tear of working with traumatised children.

When children's responses to traumatic events are unresolved, the long-term consequences may interfere with a child's ability to function emotionally, socially, academically and personally. Helping children grow through their grief requires an understanding of trauma, children's grief responses and the interaction between trauma and grief. Consequently caregivers need to be prepared to address both the post-traumatic elements of the loss and the loss-related elements.

It is beyond the scope of this book and our own expertise to attempt to give detailed accounts of the manifold causes of Post-Traumatic Stress Disorder (PTSD) in children. We do not know all the answers because each traumatic event carries with it a special burden about which our experience may not qualify us to write. We have however attempted to review some of the existing literature and to synthesize aspects of the research into children's recovery from trauma. We have sought to achieve this in a way that extends the knowledge of colleagues who have already worked with traumatised children and informs newcomers to the subject. The book does not pretend to be a definitive work: there will be those readers who are committed to working equally creatively and originally in different ways.

The text is not intended to provide guidance in the psychological or psychoanalytical theory of trauma counselling. It is first and foremost a practical text with practical ideas. Your own personal or professional experience or training may have taught you to interact with children and families in ways which are specific to their needs. Developing our own skills and capacities is good. It is impossible to provide guidelines which will fit all situations. Nevertheless, we hope the ideas expressed in this book will be useful and interesting to you.

The United Nations Convention on the Rights of the Child defines a child as someone under the age of eighteen. Throughout the book the words, child, pupil and young people are used interchangeably to cover the chronological age ranges of those who might still be in full-time schooling. Rather than using combined personal pronouns such as s/he, his/hers, which are not congruous with the way in which we speak, we sometimes use personal pronouns which relate to the male gender and sometimes those which relate to the female. We also recognise that many adults act in caring roles or are part of extended families. Therefore the term 'parents' does not refer exclusively to biological parents.

All the children's names used within the text are pseudonyms although their stories are true and the way in which they are told is unchanged. We have drawn them from our experience as teachers, counsellors, carers and practitioners in the field of grief, loss and trauma. Their personal accounts give touching insights into a world which is often overlooked.

Chapter 1 introduces the reader to the background of PTSD as a recognised condition, with particular reference to the persistent and intense effects of trauma on children. The second chapter charts the chronology of disasters during the last three and a half decades and provides an insight into the growing understanding of PTSD in survivors. Chapter 3 extends the readers understanding of the myriad of human responses to trauma illustrated by case studies and examples of children's artwork.

It is estimated about one in every ten children has suffered abuse. Chapter 4 considers categories of abuse as described by the Children Act 1989. The traumatic effects of maltreatment, neglect and separation on individual children's holistic development are discussed.

Adjusting to bereavement through death may be extraordinarily difficult for children and young people, especially if they are unable to make sense of the event or if adults 'disenfranchise' their grief. Chapter 5 considers children's responses to untimely, violent, traumatic and multiple deaths, with particular attention to anticipated and sudden family bereavement. Strategies for supporting children are discussed, including ways of including them at funerals. The following chapter extends the reader's insight into children's grief through a consideration of their developmental understanding and adjustment to chronic illness or life-threatening conditions. Attention is paid to meeting the needs of individual family members.

Chapter 7 discusses aspects of race, ethnicity, culture, religion and spirituality that should be addressed by schools and caring services, with particular reference to trauma, which results in death.

The penultimate chapter considers recovery from PTSD and argues for consideration to be given to each individual during the time they incorporate the event of the trauma into their lives. A 'snakes and ladders' model of recovery is reintroduced. Finally in Chapter 9 we urge schools to plan a framework for crisis management that acknowledges the needs of individuals and their community. We make a plea for adults to listen to what individual children are able to communicate about their needs.

Helping young people make tragic situations more tolerable is challenging and rewarding. Through caring we gain a deeper insight into the meaning of life and we renew our determination to care again. We hope you will be inspired to travel alongside children and their families as they journey through the rough terrain of life.

Erica Brown and David Kinchin
Birmingham/Oxford
January 2001

CHAPTER 1

Children and trauma: an introduction to PTSD

Traumatic events strike unexpectedly, turning everyday experiences upside-down. They destroy the belief that *'it could never happen to me'*. The impact and the human response to any event which is unexpected, violent or otherwise, is as horrific as it appears to the individual person at the time and in the days and weeks which follow. In the aftermath of a disaster people may believe that they were in the wrong place at the wrong time. The authors of this book do not adhere with the philosophy that it is only survivors of major disasters who suffer trauma. Once a person has experienced trauma it may be extremely difficult to believe that life can ever be the same again. Survival is not just to do with living – it is to do with the quality of life.

Research demonstrates that adults are deeply moved by their exposure to agonising, life-threatening events. It should come as no surprise that children's resilience is challenged as they struggle to understand and respond to traumatic events. Despite this great need to provide understanding and support for traumatised children, the literature and information available to professionals is sparse and camouflaged within the abyss of general research and study. This book sets out to provide information and guidance to teachers, professionals, carers and parents who deal with traumatised children; it also strives to provide these supportive carers with strategies to sustain them in their work.

The literature

In recent years there has been a wealth of literature which has documented disasters, and accidental deaths but with the exception of a few writers (Kinchin 1998, Rando 1993, Raphael 1986, Redmond 1989) interests in the effects of trauma on people's lives (and particularly the lives of children) has been extremely limited. Rando says that it is this incomplete perspective that has contributed to a persistence in complications, preventing victims adjusting to trauma.

Post-Traumatic Stress Disorder (PTSD) in adults has been recognised for some years. In contrast, far less has been written about the responses of children to trauma. Indeed, prior to the work of Garmezy and Rutter (1985) there was little attention paid to children's reactions to trauma. It was assumed that young people's adverse reactions were short-lived. This failure to recognise the extent of children's responses has largely been for three reasons. Firstly, because the use of generalised screening tests did not identify childhood responses and secondly, because primary carers and professional persons tended to underestimate the extent of childhood disturbances. Thirdly, emotional 'numbing' is often difficult to detect in children. In recent years this view has been revised as more children who have experienced trauma have been the subject of research studies.

Indeed, formal recognition of children's suffering of PTSD was made by the American Psychiatric Association's *Diagnostic and Statistical Manual* 1987 (see References section). In 1993 Udwin advocated more information was needed about the range of different reactions of PTSD in children and the likely duration of their responses. At the beginning of the new millennium it is widely accepted that the effects of trauma on children are very similar to responses shown by adults. There is an increased recognition of the intensity and persistence of children's traumatic responses (Yule and Williams 1990).

It should however be remembered that not all children will suffer PTSD after a trauma. Other disorders such as anxiety disorder, depression and phobias are also commonly experienced.

In school

Schools may be excellent at celebrating joyful events and special achievements but often they have greater difficulty handling children's feelings of anger, sadness and guilt. Furthermore, the emotional effects of trauma on children and adolescents may not be immediately obvious to parents or school staff. Children often try to protect adults by hiding their feelings of distress. But in some cases, the effects of the trauma may last months or years, significantly affecting pupil's academic attainment (Yule and Udwin 1991).

Like adults, children may worry that they are going mad when they start experiencing some of the symptoms associated with reliving a trauma when, in fact, they actually are suffering from PTSD (Kinchin 1998).

The history of PTSD

Since the nineteenth century, and the advent of railways, researchers have been aware of the lasting effects of traumatic events in people's lives. In 1866 trauma was described as 'railway spine' when survivors of a rail crash showed symptoms. Since then, the names attached to traumatic reactions have changed to suit the circumstances of the events and many of the terms have related to military combat. 'Nervous shock' and 'traumatic neuroses' were terms used at the end of the nineteenth century and these were followed by labels such as 'fright neuroses' and 'shell-shock' to describe victims of warfare and disaster.

The term 'shell-shock' was most commonly associated with the Great War of 1914–18. Originally it referred to the belief that combat-related disorder was caused by minute brain haemorrhages occurring as the result of excessive exposure to explosions and bomb blasts. Observations that soldiers could develop shell-shock even in the absence of explosions, led to the belief that shell-shock implied a weakness of character with the consequence that many soldiers of the Great War (who today would have been diagnosed as suffering from PTSD) were executed for cowardice. Very recently some survivors have been pardoned and a diagnosis PTSD has been recognised. Nevertheless, the suggestion that PTSD may be attributed to character weakness has lingered in the minds of some people. More than eighty years after the Great War some PTSD sufferers still fear they are being labelled as weak and cowardly.

By the Second World War a more detailed description of post-traumatic stress was considered by psychiatrists. However, there were still a wide variety of names used to describe the disorder including post trauma syndrome, traumatophobia and war neurosis. Moreover, civilians were also seen to be suffering similar symptoms following events which had nothing to do with combat.

The battle for full recognition and understanding of what PTSD was about continued well into the 1960s and 1970s and the Vietnam War. It was this theatre of war, and the high number of traumatised combat troops, which provided the impetus for the current interest in Post-Traumatic Stress Disorder. A definition of the condition appeared in a US diagnostic and statistical manual of mental disorders (DSM) in 1980. The definition was revised in 1987, and again in 1994 (DSM–IV). This book is largely concerned with the increased understanding of the effects of PTSD from 1994 onwards.

Progression of PTSD by definition, through Diagnostic and Statistical Manuals

- DSM I   1952   'Gross Stress Reaction'
- DSM II   1968   'Adjustment Reaction to Adult Life'
- DSM III   1980   'Post-Traumatic Stress Disorder' (following the Vietnam War)
- DSM IIIR   1987   'Post-Traumatic Stress Disorder' (enhanced the 1980 definition and added the 'one month' criterion and suggested that children might be affected.)
- DSM IV   1994   'Post-Traumatic Stress Disorder' (a shift in the thinking of what can be considered 'traumatic' allowed for the individual person's perception of the event to add a subjectivity to the traumatic nature of any situation).

PTSD and children

The first in-depth study of the effects of trauma on children was undertaken as recently as 1979. The studies by Lenore Terr (1981) focused on a group of 26 children aged between 5 and 14 years who were kidnapped while on their school bus.

More recent commentators have suggested that children suffer far more violent victimisations than adults do (Calouste Gulbenkian Foundation 1995). Their uniquely dependent status renders them more vulnerable to conventional crimes such as murder and assault; to family violence including violent punishments, sexual abuse and assaults by siblings; to institutional violence and particularly to bullying in schools. There are also marked gender differences: boys are more vulnerable than girls to physical abuse and non-family assaults, while girls are three times as likely to be sexually abused (Creighton 1992, NSPCC 1995).

PTSD – the definition

Six criteria need to be met before a diagnosis of Post-Traumatic Stress Disorder can be made.

1. The person must have been exposed to a traumatic event or events that involve actual or threatened death or serious injury, or threat to the physical integrity of themselves or others. The person's response must involve fear, helplessness or horror.
2. The traumatic event must be persistently relived by the person.
3. The person must persistently avoid stimuli associated with the trauma.
4. The person must experience symptoms of increased arousal, or over-awareness, not present before the trauma.
5. The disturbance must cause significant distress or impairment in social, occupational, or other areas of functioning important to the person.
6. Symptoms, linked to 2, 3 and 4 above, must last more than one month.

When are events described as traumatic?

The most obvious causes of trauma are accidents and incidents which cause physical injury to people. A road accident may well be responsible for physical injuries. The same incident may also cause psychological injuries which are unrecognised by everyone except the victim of the trauma.

Maxim's story. I saw my cousin on a life support machine. His face was white and kind of transparent. He was eleven and I was eight. The night I saw him I had a terrible scary dream about the way he looked. I wish someone had told me what to expect and also that I would never see him alive again. I am glad I saw him but it would have been good if my uncle had asked me if I wanted to go before I got to the hospital.

Common stressors causing PTSD in children

Four types of situations are the most likely stressors:

- Serious threat or harm to the child's life.
- Serious threat or harm to a child's loved ones.
- Sudden destruction of the child's home or community.
- Seeing another person who is being or has been recently seriously injured or killed as the result of an accident or physical violence.

Incidents which can traumatise

Incidents which can traumatise adults and children can be divided into five groups:

- criminal incidents – assaults, burglary, robbery, kidnapping, terrorism;
- accidents – at home, on the roads, at school;
- abuse – sexual, emotional, physical, bullying;
- natural disasters – floods, land slips, freak weather conditions;
- major disasters – train and plane crashes, ships sinking, acts of war.

This is not an exhaustive list and does not include such extreme cases as the Chernobyl nuclear accident, or the Hillsborough stadium disaster. Neither does it recognise incidents which have not previously been associated with PTSD such as poor school inspection results or a drop in student examination grades. Any incident responsible for causing the sequelae of criteria listed above can be described as a traumatic incident.

Death caused by accidents, disasters, war, suicide or murder qualify as traumatic stressors. For some children reactions will be minimal or short-lived depending on factors such as individual personality, shortened exposure to the event or support from older persons. Circumstances associated with severe reactions include:

- the suddenness of the event;
- the severity of threat to life;
- the degree to which the child was rendered powerless during the trauma;
- the intensity, proximity and duration of exposure to the imagery involved.

Pre-existing vulnerability from earlier trauma may also have a part to play, but complications do not inevitably occur. Some commentators have suggested that those children and adolescents previously thought to be suffering from attention deficit hyperactivity disorder (ADHD), conduct disorder, or substance abuse disorders may be at greatest risk of being traumatised (Dwivedi 2000).

Over time many symptoms of PTSD fluctuate in severity but they may persist for weeks or months. Anniversaries or stressful times such as examinations may exacerbate difficulties. Sleep disturbances are common in children suffering PTSD. They include:

- problems getting to sleep;
- frequent awakening;
- night terrors;
- fear of being alone;
- fear of the dark.

Children and trauma

The events described in the next chapter would cause adults deep distress. Some anecdotal evidence suggests that children recover from trauma more speedily than adults. Somehow it is felt that the invisible injury brought about is less serious if the victim is a child. Advocates of this view claim that children very quickly convert from being victims to being survivors. There is, however, no reliable research to support this anecdotal view and our experience does not support it because the evidence to substantiate that hope is absent.

Moreover, research suggests that children need more, not less, understanding and care. Following the Chowchilla kidnapping in 1976 (see Chapter 2) the psychiatrist dealing with the victims reported that all 26 children exhibited significant post-traumatic effects (Terr 1983). Following major disasters at Aberfan (Lacey 1972) and at Buffalo Creek (James et al. 1976) large numbers of children required help and guidance for at least two years following the events. Other researchers have suggested that traumatised children may be affected in a variety of ways. Most commonly the effects may be exhibited as illnesses, absences from school, learning difficulties, lack of academic achievement and poor development (McFarlane and Blumbergs 1985). More detailed accounts of how PTSD affects people are discussed in later chapters.

Children's stress responses

Although stress reactions in children are complex, they are in fact normal human responses to unanticipated and sudden and frightening events. The world has become unpredictable and routines have been shattered. For young people who experience any kind of abuse, everyday events are turned into nightmares which do not cease at daybreak. Rather they continue in some cases for many months and years. Like the adult who has to contend with the experiences of trauma, children struggle with the agonising experiences and often with the search for the unanswerable questions of 'why me?' and 'who or what am I now?' or 'what will I become as I continue to encounter intense and unexpected emotions?' Confusion and disorganisation turns life upside down.

In some cases the nature of the trauma seems to determine the nature of the stress experience. Research suggests that if the trauma involves heat or noise or darkness children may suffer more intense reactions. Likewise bereavement, personal injury or threat to life may cause particularly severe traumatic responses. Other important elements such as the duration of the exposure to the trauma, whether the event was experienced in isolation or with other persons, and the possibility of reoccurrence play a significant part in individual children's reactions.

Imagery

Imagery of the event seems to 'condense' the experience in a way that emphasises the most horrendous memories. For example Jason was asleep in his bedroom the night his parents' thatched cottage caught alight. He recalls,

> I still smell the straw and the wood burning and I can remember my Mum screaming my name. When the fireman rescued me I saw everything from my home eaten up by the fire and there were big bubbles of liquid plastic coming out of the sofa like a volcano.

Four years after the event he could not tolerate the smell of toast cooking or the sound of a fire engine siren. Media coverage of bush fires in Montana in 2000 triggered nightmares for Jason.

Survivor guilt

Survivor guilt after major disasters has been studied by authors such as Hodgkinson and Stewart (1991), Lifton (1983) and Pynoos (1992). Lifton distinguishes between *animating guilt* where people feel a responsibility towards those who did not survive and *static guilt* where the sense of responsibility prevents the person from moving on. For young people who have experienced aggressive or destructive feelings towards siblings or adults in the past, there may be a sense that these feelings implicated the event or trauma in which other people suffered. Young people who have been the victims of abuse may attach self-blame to what happened and this is often accompanied by fierce self-accusation.

Denial and numbing

Many children will experience a phase of denial and numbing as an initial response after a stressful event has occurred. After this phase the child is confronted with intrusive, repetitive recollections of the event which may alternate with denial and numbing. It has been argued that this alternation of phases is a way in which children manage the power of their emotions and that it continues until the traumatic event is worked through (Rando 1993).

Searching for meaning

All survivors of trauma need to make sense of their experience. For children there will be questions such as:

- Why did it happen to me?
- Why did I survive?
- Why do I feel the way I do?
- Does the way I feel now reflect the person I am?

Why did it happen to me?

Many children who have been the victims of trauma believe they were in some way responsible for what happened. Thus the child who has witnessed violence in his home may perceive his behaviour contributed to the event. Others may be confused about why they were singled out to be a victim, especially if they see siblings apparently unaffected by events.

Why did I survive?

Why an individual has survived may pose a myriad of questions to which there are no definitive answers and it is these questions which often lie at the heart of survivor guilt.

Why do I feel the way I do?

Children often battle with the strength of their emotions and many may not have the language to describe levels of emotional response. Children may never have experienced intense emotions prior to the event and it is not unusual for them to attempt to repress these unknown feelings or, conversely, to perceive that they are going mad. Many do not know where they can seek help. The world is unfamiliar and frightening.

Does the way I feel now reflect the person I really am?

Life will never be the same again because whatever the trauma experienced there can be no looking back. The experience has to be incorporated into the present time and into the child's future.

Children's changed behaviour

Post traumatic stress reactions combine physical responses, behaviours and thoughts which are the result of an event which violates previously held concepts of well-being and safety. Little is known about individual differences in children's responses to trauma or the factors which can render some children more susceptible to PTSD than others. The degree of a child's exposure to a traumatic event seems to play a critical part in the severity of PTSD however (Pynoos *et al.* 1987). It is important not to make the assumption that all responses to trauma are negative ones, although according to Raphael (1986) man-made trauma may result in higher distress levels than natural disasters.

What influences a child's capacity to cope with trauma?

Before trauma a child will demonstrate individual characteristics and relatively predictable behavioural patterns which will be referred to in general terms as his or her personality. How well a child copes with trauma is dependent on several interrelating factors, some of which are like those described by Brown (1999) in respect of interrelated features of bereavement. These factors will include:

- the child's cognitive ability;
- the presence of primary carers;
- significant others in the child's life;
- the child's capacity to express emotions;
- the maintenance of familiar routines;
- the stability of home/care environment;
- levels of support from within and outside the child's home;
- culture;
- media attitudes;
- opportunities for alternative ways of behaving;
- time.

(See Figure 1.1)

Although it is unlikely that children will experience all of the following changes in behaviour, many will present with observable signs of:

- restlessness;
- irritability or outbursts of anger;
- exaggerated startle response.

Additionally if a young person encounters an event similar to an aspect of the trauma, other responses may occur, e.g. crying, screaming, or difficulty in breathing. However it should be remembered that severity of PTSD symptoms are not necessarily indicators of the severity of response to the trauma. Neither does PTSD follow a regular predictable pattern.

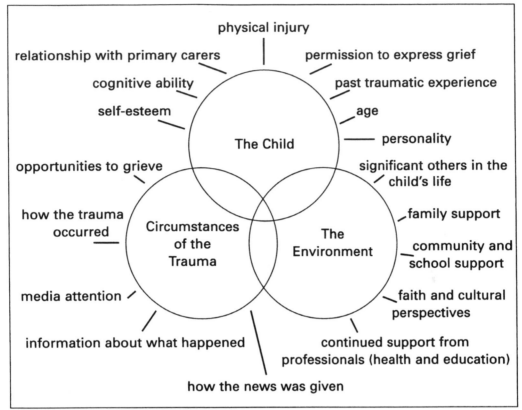

physical injury

relationship with primary carers

permission to express grief

cognitive ability

past traumatic experience

self-esteem

age

personality

The Child

opportunities to grieve

significant others in the child's life

how the trauma occurred

Circumstances of the Trauma

The Environment

family support

community and school support

media attention

faith and cultural perspectives

information about what happened

continued support from professionals (health and education)

how the news was given

Figure 1.1 Interrelating features of trauma

Individual responses

From a very early age children strive to make sense of the world in which they live. In the time which follows a traumatic event, one task towards recovery will be what Horowitz (1978) calls 'cognitive completion'. The completion involves the integration of the experience into the child's view of the world in which they lived in the past and will continue to live in the future. Smith (1986) refers to this as 'weaving each strand of the experience into the fabric of the child's life'.

Some studies have examined the influence of race, age and gender on children's responses to trauma but the findings are inconsistent (Lonigan *et al.* 1991, Green *et al.* 1991). Burke *et al.* (1982) found children with special educational needs were more likely to show increased behavioural problems following trauma, whilst Tsui (1991) reported able pupils involved in the sinking of the cruise ship 'Jupiter' less likely to develop PTSD. However, it should be noted, the latter group performed academically less well post disaster.

The most influential factor in children's responses to disaster appears to relate to parental reactions with an increased likelihood of children being affected where parents suffer PTSD and are unable to give support (Green *et al.* 1991). Likewise the adjustment of children contributes to the overall adjustment of the family.

Two aspects of children's behaviour are particularly worth considering. These are re-experience of the event and avoidance behaviour.

Re-experiencing the event

In children this may be manifested through:

- repetitive play in which the event is expressed in role play or through the use of representative objects;
- recurrent nightmares which feature the event;
- flashbacks of the event during the day;
- distress when partaking in or being exposed to situations which resemble aspects of the event, including sensory experiences.

These events may 'trigger' the memory of the original trauma.

Avoidance behaviour

Children may show avoidance of activities and situations associated with the trauma or objects which were present at the time. Sometimes they also avoid recalling the event. Avoidance behaviour may be manifested through:

- lack of interest in normal activities;
- loss of previously mastered skills, e.g. language or toileting;
- feelings of detachment from primary carers/siblings;
- inability to form relationships;
- fear of the future and adulthood.

Children's concept of time changes with age and so does their comprehension of the trauma. They have a continuing need to make sense of what has happened which may mean regular review of the facts. As their thinking and adaptation to trauma develops this in turns brings new information, needs and possibly changed fears.

What does the child need?

Children will require:

- opportunities to form a trusting relationship with supportive carers;
- accessible and easily understood information which affirms recognition of PTSD;
- skilled professional intervention which focuses on symptoms, behaviours and support where the trauma is recalled;
- appropriate acceptance of the helplessness and powerlessness expressed during the trauma;
- help to integrate traumatic events into a new identity and an affirmation of positive self-image;
- access to treatment where necessary;
- permission to reach a resolution to their grief and to move on.

For many children the pain and difficulties associated with trauma are not recognised or shared with the result that their grief may take years to resolve. The child may be surrounded by family and friends who are also grieving or familiar people may be absent altogether which adds to feelings of insecurity. The long-term support of such children should be a continuation of the care given at the time of the crisis. However, before adults can begin to help children they need to have confronted their own experiences and emotions in order that they are in touch with the bereaved child within themselves.

Approaches to treatment of PTSD

Appropriate and successful strategies for the treatment of children with PTSD are not widely reported but the work of Yule and Udwin (1991) and Pynoos and Nader (1998) is helpful in providing some clinical examples of effective debriefing after disasters. Yule and Udwin advocate that children need to review their experiences in a supportive and secure environment where they are able to express their emotions. McFarlane and Blumbergs (1985) acknowledge the reluctance which many people have towards therapy or treatment.

Approaches to treatment of PTSD will be discussed later in the book, but they include:

- group therapy or family therapy;
- cognitive behaviour techniques;
- debriefing;
- writing detailed accounts of the event;
- drawing events;
- role play.

PTSD – secondary victims

So far, we have introduced the possibility of PTSD affecting primary victims or those directly involved in a traumatic situation. However, children may witness a trauma, and become traumatised as a consequence. This act of witnessing does not not have to be in the conventional understanding of the term, e.g. if a child is sitting at home watching television and suddenly sees news footage of an event, such as the Hillsborough disaster, and knows her father or brother is at that football match then that child can become a secondary victim of PTSD.

Furthermore, a child who did not actually witness the event firsthand or in the media could still be traumatised if another family member is suffering. Witnessing a close family member with traumatic symptoms, such as panic attacks or flashbacks, may be sufficient to induce a post traumatic reaction in other family members.

PTSD – tertiary victims

Witnessing a traumatic event that involves complete strangers can be traumatic. In extreme cases children (and adults) who have witnessed an event as a casual observer have developed PTSD symptoms.

Summary

Whether children witness a traumatic event firsthand, or in other circumstances, there is no doubt that children can be traumatised and the effects of the traumatic reaction can adversely affect their academic achievement and their social behaviour in school. Exactly how children might be affected and what can be done to minimalise the effects is discussed in later chapters of this book.

CHAPTER 2

Traumatic events involving children

Over the years there have been many events which have resulted in significant numbers of children being traumatised. Each large-scale event attracted immense media attention at the time but eventually the interest waned and those who were affected were abandoned by the media. They were of no further interest.

However, those traumatised by these events continued to suffer from the aftershocks of the trauma and carried traumatic scar tissue for the rest of their lives. In order to chart the progress that has been made in understanding Post-Traumatic Stress Disorder it may be useful to examine the following events:

> **Aberfan, 21 October 1966** – pre knowledge of PTSD (Austin 1967, Lacey 1972, Miller 1974, Raphael 1986)
>
> **Buffalo Creek, 26 February 1972** – first modern study of the effects of trauma (Cohen 1991, Erikson 1976, Green 1991, James *et al.* 1976, Stern 1976)
>
> **Chowchilla, 15 July 1976** – first study of children and PTSD (Raphael 1986, Saylor 1993, Terr 1981, 1983)
>
> *Jupiter*, **21 October 1988** – children from 20 schools traumatised (Yule and Williams 1990, and Udwin 1991, and Gold 1993, Yule 1999)
>
> **Swindon, 25 January 1990** – a school based trauma (Parker *et al.* 1995, Randall and Parker 1997)
>
> **Dunblane, 13 March 1996** – PTSD well understood by this time (Randall and Parker 1997)
>
> **Wasserbillig, 31 May 2000** – child hostages in day-care centre (Osborn 2000).

Aberfan

Friday, 21 October 1966, was the last school day before half-term. The weather was depressingly misty but the children and staff at Pantglas Junior School, in Aberfan, were all looking forward to the brief holiday (Austin 1967). 240 boys and girls made their way to school. The youngest was four and a half, and the eldest was eleven. Pantglas was a happy school and most of the parents of Aberfan had known it as children themselves; they had learned their first lessons within its well-built brick and stone walls. This is what happened.

09.15 School has settled down. The teacher is about to mark the register. A call of 'dinner children', is heard from the corridor. Some go to pay their dinner shillings in the hall. Two are spotted by the headmistress, Miss Jennings, and sent to the senior school with a message.

09.18 An avalanche crashes through the school. It kills one of the two children on their way to the senior school. A black, wet mass slurps through a classroom, and fills Miss Jennings' study. She's 64, due to retire at the end of term. Next door to her Mrs Bates and 33 children, aged 10 and 11, all die.

09.29 All 11 of the school soccer team, who had won their match against Troedyrhiw Junior School 3–2 the afternoon before, are killed.

A waste tip had slid down the side of the valley and demolished several houses and the school. The incident at Aberfan, in South Wales, killed 116 children and 28 adults. In just fourteen minutes every person in the community had been permanently scarred by a disaster which touched the hearts of millions (Miller 1974).

This disaster is vividly recalled by many Britons because it was covered by television crews who arrived on the scene. The full horror and traumatic consequences of the disaster were screened in millions of homes. The first news flash was broadcast on radio at 10.30 a.m. It brought reporters by the dozen, and television services for the first big outside broadcast disaster coverage in TV history.

In 1966 nobody talked about Post-Traumatic Stress Disorder. Nobody understood about the affects of trauma on children, or parents, or the rescuers (Lacey 1972). People coped as best they could, and while the nation watched on TV, the community of Aberfan started to pick up the pieces of their lives.

Summary:

- 144 fatalities;
- duration of traumatic incident – 20 minutes;
- heavily covered by mass media, particularly television.

Buffalo Creek

On Saturday, 26 February 1972, an enormous slag dam gave way and unleashed thousands of tons of water and black mud on the Buffalo Creek valley in southern West Virginia. The mining hamlets of Becco and Pardee and the town of Saunders were almost totally destroyed. The disaster resulted in 126 deaths, and it left 4,000 people homeless. Many of the dead were women and children. Like the Aberfan tragedy, the actual incident lasted a short time, 20 minutes, but the consequences were devastating (Erikson 1976).

Adults and children who survived referred to the disaster as 'the end of time' or 'the end of everything', and claimed that 'no one who was not there could ever really know what it was like' (James *et al.* 1976). Victims were haunted by visual memories of the event as they struggled with the emotional guilt and the drowning of relatives and friends and witnessing blackened bodies that were uncovered for weeks after the flood. For these communities, the impossible had happened.

The shock was overwhelming and an outlook of pessimism, emptiness and hopelessness dominated the region. Such comments as 'nothing counts anymore' and 'what's the use of anything?' became common. Survivors felt guilt for having survived. Anxiety, depression and feelings of inadequacy were commonplace.

In 1966, the people of Aberfan were considered to be suffering from 'severe shock'. In 1972, those in Buffalo Creek were labelled as suffering from a 'complex' which became journalistically known as 'Buffalo Creek Syndrome'. Traumatic reactions were found in 80 per cent of the survivors of the Buffalo Creek disaster and many victims were still left psychologically scarred two years after the event.

Summary:

- 126 fatalities, 4,000 people made homeless;
- duration of traumatic incident – 20 minutes;
- survivors suffered 'Buffalo Creek Syndrome'.

Chowchilla

On Thursday, 15 July 1976, 26 children who had enrolled in the Alview Dairyland Summer School, Chowchilla, California, were kidnapped. The children, aged 5 to 14 years, were travelling in a bus when three masked men stopped it at gun point. The children were transferred to two vans which were driven for about 11 hours before they were transferred again to a 'hole in the ground' which was later found to be a buried truck trailer. The group spent 16 hours inside this buried trailer until two of the oldest boys managed to dig themselves out. This was no 20-minute-trauma. The group had suffered a 27 hour ordeal.

Immediately after the event, when the children had been reunited with their parents and friends, a meeting was arranged for the parents to speak with a specialist mental health centre physician. This man told the children's parents that he confidently predicted only 1 in 26 of the children would be emotionally affected by the experience.

Parents were naturally reluctant to admit their child was affected. Consequently there was a time lag of over five months before families started asking for help. When psychiatrist Lenore Terr met with the 23 children (who remained living in Chowchilla six months after the event) she concluded that all those she interviewed were severely traumatised (Terr 1981, 1983).

The Chowchilla incident was significantly different to the disasters at Aberfan and Buffalo Creek. Firstly, the trauma lasted many hours compared to just a few minutes. Secondly, the group consisted of children only. Thirdly, there were no fatalities.

Researchers were keen to examine the children of Chowchilla and to explore their understanding of trauma. Four years after the incident all 23 children were interviewed by Terr and her team, and all continued to exhibit some signs of the trauma. This included one child who had been let off the bus moments before the kidnapping. He was traumatised by the event (even though he was not kidnapped) and by the police interview conducted immediately after the incident.

Many of the strategies used to treat traumatised children today are based on the research undertaken of the children who were kidnapped from the school bus.

Summary:

- no fatalities – hostage situation;
- duration of traumatic event – over 27 hours;
- first study into the effects of trauma on children.

Jupiter

In March 1987 the *Herald of Free Enterprise* sank off the Belgian coast with the loss of 192 lives. This disaster was widely covered by television news. Just 19 months later, on Friday, 21 October 1988, the cruise ship *Jupiter* sank while carrying children from 20 different schools. On the *Herald of Free Enterprise* the surviving children were unknown to each other but on the *Jupiter* some of the children were in groups of 30 from the same school. One school had to cope with the death of a pupil, another suffered the death of a teacher. Every one of the schools involved had to deal with significant numbers of severely traumatised teenage children.

Following incidents such as the sinking of the *Herald of Free Enterprise*, the public and support services became much more aware of the affects of trauma. Despite this, many basic mistakes were made with the youngsters who were traumatised on the *Jupiter*.

In a girls' school one of the privileges of being in Year 11 was girls could sit on the balcony during assembly (Yule and Gold 1993). The balcony was steeply raked and had a small iron railing at the bottom of the steps. The balcony bore a remarkable similarity to the deck of a sinking ship and yet it took teachers many weeks to find a reason for the reluctance of some girls to attend assembly.

> One girl was late into a class during a very wet day and complained that the teacher ignored her plight. She was referring to the fact that she had to sit in wet clothes which acted as a memory trigger and reminded her of the time she spent sitting in wet clothing at the quay side at Piraeus after being rescued from the *Jupiter*. She suffered flashbacks of the original trauma. It was probably not an obvious connection for the teacher to have to make, but for the child concerned it was extremely retraumatising.

At another school the survivors of the *Jupiter* sinking were all geography students. When the pupils attended their first lesson they encountered a wall display on the subject 'Great Disasters of the World'. Tragically, the sinking of the *Titanic* was one of the disasters illustrated. A school who sent pupils on the *Jupiter* noticed that those girls who had asked to go on the cruise but were not awarded places were more affected after the disaster than those who never expressed any interest in the cruise (Yule and Gold 1993). A final piece of research linked to this incident examined the affects of trauma on exam results. A comparison was made, in one school, between the end of year results for three previous years, and for the year of the *Jupiter* sinking. (The exams came ten months after the sinking.) In this school, the girls taking the exam were slightly more able than the rest of their year group. By comparing them with 24 other pupils matched for their levels of achievement prior to the incident, it was observed that the sinking had a significant effect on their school performance. This effect continued into Year 11 and resulted in lower GCSE results than had originally been predicted.

Summary:

- four fatalities, duration of the trauma – many hours;
- closely followed the *Herald of Free Enterprise* sinking;
- large quantity of research followed this incident.

Swindon

On Friday, 25 January 1990, just as children were settling down to lessons after lunch, a hurricane force wind hit Swindon and the roof of a junior school was blown off. One class of 30 (Year 6) children was directly affected by this event. One child was killed and another suffered serious leg injuries.

The children were evacuated to a nearby community hall to await collection by their parents. Many of the parents heard of the tragedy by word of mouth or on the local radio. They knew a child had been killed but they did not know the child's name. A few parents went to collect their children from school at the normal time, only to discover the school building was wrecked.

The effects of this disaster were not studied until one of the children was referred to a Child Guidance Clinic 14 months after the incident. Of the 29 pupils left in the class in which the child was killed, 19 agreed to be interviewed and become part of the study. Eight boys and 11 girls were interviewed at home by Parker, Watts and Allsopp, approximately two years after the incident.

Separate interviews were carried out with the child and one parent in each family. Each child was asked to complete an Impact of Events Questionnaire (IOE) on two occasions; once shortly after the incident and once during the week before the interview. None of the children experienced any difficulty remembering how they had felt at the time of the incident, despite the length of time which had elapsed. Each child's parent was also asked to complete the same questionnaire shortly after the incident, together with a version of the General Health Questionnaire which was designed to assess their well-being.

The results of the IOE were significant with the children *and the parents* exhibiting a serious degree of traumatisation. The mean score for the children two years after the incident still reflected significant levels of anxiety.

A few children recognised that their parents showed significant changes in their behaviour. In one case a father demonstrated uncharacteristic angry outbursts following everyday stress (e.g. the car not starting) for several months after the event. In another a mother checked the weather forecast several times a day and tried to make her children stay at home if high winds were predicted. Another father spent the 36 hours following the incident completing work on an extension he was building, so that his family would be safe.

Parents noticed changes in their children: eight reported behavioural problems; ten reported emotional difficulties. Sleep disturbances were very common (16 cases). Parents reported child sleeping in their room (three cases), the child moving to a bottom bunk (two cases), a radio or light being left on in the child's bedroom (four cases), the child sleeping downstairs (three cases) and the whole family sleeping together (one case). Nine of the parents thought their child avoided talking about the incident and the same number reported their children becoming upset during discussions which related to the trauma.

The findings of the Swindon research are significant because they document information about the post-traumatic reactions of parents and children following a disaster. None of the parents had been directly involved in the event, yet it would appear that the traumatic stress reactions could be accurately recalled – two years after the disaster.

Analysis of data from the children showed that they too recalled significant stress reactions. Those who were close friends of the dead child developed more symptoms of PTSD than the other children. These findings suggest that it was the experience of loss that contributed to their PTSD as well as being exposed to personal danger.

The parents suffered stress reactions of very similar severity to their children even though their stressor was different. The children were traumatised by the roof falling on them but they knew they were safe very quickly after the event. The parents, on the other hand, were not present. They heard the news on the radio or from a friend. They endured an agonising wait before they received news of survivors. Some had seen the wrecked school before learning that their child was safe. For most of the children the exposure to traumatic stress was limited to five minutes. For the parents the exposure to traumatic stress was, on average, five or six times longer.

It is significant that a great majority of the children found their parents' behaviour appropriate and helpful. For those children who found their parent's behaviour less helpful they cited parental lack of communication as a problem.

Summary:

- one fatality;
- duration of the traumatic incident – a few minutes;
- research focused on children and their parents.

Dunblane

On Wednesday, 13 March 1996, the world was shocked by the shooting incident which occurred in the small town of Dunblane. A 43-year-old man calmly walked into a school and shot dead 16 children and their teacher. Plenty of debate ensued about why someone should do such a thing, and why so many guns were available to Hamilton. The country's gun laws were changed as a direct result of the incident.

The incident lasted only 20 minutes but affected a great number of people (Randall and Parker 1997), not least the remaining 700 children and teachers at the school. Children and teachers at hundreds of other schools realised that the incident could easily have happened to their community. Emergency service staff and support staff who treated the families were also traumatised. In short, the shooting affected hundreds of people in different ways.

Summary:

- 17 fatalities, in a short space of time;
- the incident was perceived as wholly preventable;
- psychologists recognised the significance of the 'trauma bond'.

Wasserbillig, Luxembourg

On Wednesday, 31 May 2000, a lone gunman walked into a day-care centre in a sleepy border town with a population of just 2,300 people. He took more than 40 adults and children hostage and threatened to kill them with the gun, grenade and knife that he carried. Slowly, hostages were released but after 30 hours 25 children (mostly under four years old) and three adults were still being held against their will.

The 39-year-old gunman had a history of mental illness. A very unstable hostage situation remained keenly balanced until a police marksman was able to shoot the hostage taker and free all the hostages unharmed (Osborn 2000).

This incident illustrates how traumatic life-threatening situations can occur in any location and at any time – often when they are least expected. At Wasserbillig teams of counsellors and psychologists were on hand to offer help and assistance to the families of the hostages even before the event had been concluded. Perhaps the lessons from earlier incidents, such as Chowchilla which was a similar kidnapping event, have now been learned.

Summary:

- no fatalities, duration of the incident – over 30 hours;
- psychologists on scene to support parents and staff;
- too soon for any research to be carried out, and published.

The tragedies of Dunblane and Aberfan are separated by 30 years, and 315 miles, but the people involved became united by the bond which unites all those who have experienced a traumatic event – an event which has a profound effect on the lives of all it touches.

A great deal has been learned since the mud slide at Aberfan in 1966. The tragedies at Buffalo Creek, Chowchilla, the *Jupiter*, Swindon, Dunblane and Wasserbillig demonstrate how large-scale traumatic events have affected schools and the communities served by those schools. Each of the events is quite different, and they span one third of a century. During the time which has elapsed our understanding of trauma, traumatic stress, and post-traumatic stress disorder has grown substantially.

However, these incidents have been headline news in the media. They have drawn the attention of the public and, in consequence, the support and interest of caring professionals and researchers. Large-scale traumas are well documented. Smaller traumatic events in which perhaps only one or two people are involved happen every day. Road accidents, accidents at school or work, sudden deaths due to illness, suicides, rapes, instances of abuse or bullying, happen in small communities throughout the world. Individually, they may appear to have minimal impact but combined they have a far greater impact than any shooting or mud slide or boat sinking.

In the Introduction to this book, David's story recalls a small-scale tragic event. Thomas and Taya were only two of the 8,500 children under 15 years of age who were either killed or seriously injured in road traffic accidents in Great Britain during 1987. Around the country there were thousands of similar accidents which affected children, their families and their schools. Statistically, one third of Britain's schools had experience of at least one pupil being involved in such a road accident. Since 1987, the number of serious road accidents has declined, but it is anticipated that over 6,000 children will be killed or seriously injured on British roads during 2001–02 (HMSO *Social Trends* 1998).

Research into the traumatic consequences of road traffic accidents has been undertaken by a number of bodies including the Oxford Road Accident Group (ORAG). ORAG looked at 188 consecutive road accident victims admitted to the John Radcliffe Hospital following 184 different road accidents (Mayou *et al.* 1993). The victims were interviewed a year after the accidents and it was found that over ten per cent were suffering from PTSD symptoms. The researchers concluded that psychiatric symptoms were frequent after major and less severe road accident injuries. It further concluded that PTSD symptoms were both common and disabling.

Summary

This chapter has provided a brief résumé of the nature of trauma which may affect children. The chronology of disasters from Aberfan to Wasserbillig shows an understanding of how disasters affect people. It is the large-scale traumatic incidents which attract the attention of the media, and the subsequent attentions of researchers. The inclusion of a more localised trauma which affected only a handful of people helps to identify the frequency of traumatic incidents in general. Children are very unlikely to become involved in a future disaster such as Chowchilla or Wasserbillig, but are increasingly likely to become involved in trauma such as a motoring accident or an assault. The local incidents are rarely headline material but they are sufficiently numerous on a national scale to play a significant part in our children's holistic development.

CHAPTER 3

Symptoms of Post-Traumatic Stress Disorder

Symptoms of PTSD fall into three broad groups: intrusive, avoidant and physical. Taken individually, some symptoms may appear to be simply minor irritations with no cause for concern. Taken in any combination, these same symptoms can totally destroy a child's lifestyle, friendships, education prospects and relationships at home.

Untreated these symptoms can last a lifetime. It is therefore vital that the reactions are seen for what they are: the natural consequence of being confronted with a traumatic, life-threatening event. The four types of symptom are linked closely to the diagnostic table describing PTSD which is cited in Chapter 1 and repeated here:

PTSD criteria

Six criteria need to be met before a diagnosis of
Post-Traumatic Stress Disorder can be made

1. **Trauma** – The person must be exposed to a traumatic event or events that involve actual or threatened death or serious injury, or threat to the physical integrity of himself or others. The person's response must involve fear, helplessness or horror.
2. **Intrusive** – The event must be persistently relived by the person.
3. **Avoidant** – The person must persistently avoid stimuli associated with the trauma.
4. **Physical** – The person must experience persistent symptoms of increased arousal, or 'over-awareness'.
5. **Social** – The disturbance must cause significant distress or impairment in social, occupational, or other areas of functioning important to the person.
6. **Time** – Symptoms, linked to 2, 3 and 4 above, must have lasted at least a month.

(Kinchin 1998)

Not everyone who experiences the first five criteria will be troubled by the symptoms for over a month. It is only those who continue to suffer after that period who can be confirmed as suffering from Post-Traumatic Stress Disorder.

If the disorder is successfully treated within three months, it is described as an acute case of PTSD. Over half of those initially affected have recovered three months later and can therefore be defined as acute PTSD survivors.

When the condition persists for more than three months, a person is described as suffering chronic PTSD. In these instances, the 'trauma beliefs' have become less susceptible to influence, repeated avoidance behaviour is well established, and survivors are far more likely to default from counselling. Consequently, the chronic condition is often compounded by feelings of depression and anxiety, and treatment or support becomes more difficult. In children, these compounded problems may initially be attributed to naughtiness.

When a person encounters a traumatic, life-threatening event, the brain juggles between recalling the painfulness of the event (intrusions) and going to great lengths to forget it (avoidance). The sufferer's mood will see-saw between the two. Each process has its own set of symptoms which, in turn, act as a catalyst for the physical symptoms to develop. (*Note* – There are many symptoms of Post-Traumatic Stress Disorder. Not all are experienced by every survivor.)

Intrusive

- Recurrent and distressing recollections.
- Flashbacks, thoughts, nightmares, dreams.
- Phobias, about specific daily routines, events or objects.
- Feelings of guilt for having survived.

Avoidant

- Detachment from others, emotional numbness.
- Avoidance of thoughts or feelings associated with the event.
- Markedly diminished interest or pleasure in most activities.

Physical

- Sleep problems.
- Hypervigilance.
- Exaggerated startle response.
- Joint/muscle pains.
- Feelings of nervousness.

Social

- Violent outbursts.
- Increased irritability.
- Impaired memory.
- Inability to concentrate.
- Irrational or impulsive behaviour.
- Low self-esteem.

Time

- Depression/anxiety.

Following a traumatic incident, those exposed to the trauma will start to exhibit a number of symptoms (Hamblen 1998). The symptoms will not all present themselves together – some will not appear at all. But during the weeks and months of the aftermath of a traumatic incident some symptoms may occur. They are detailed below. Each symptom is described and expressed in a way which is particularly pertinent to those caring for children and adolescents. Each symptom is like a small time bomb – circumstances or events may trigger the explosion.

☀ Recurrent and intrusive distressing recollections of the event

It is perhaps obvious, but important to stress, that the recollections of the traumatic event must be intrusive; they must be distressing, and they must be recurrent. It is not just a case of remembering what happened and becoming sad or upset by the memory. For example, a child who is quietly sitting and working on a mathematical problem may pause from the task in hand, and experience a distressing memory of the car accident he witnessed a few weeks ago. Subsequently the same child may have thoughts about the accident and start to feel guilty that it was not him that called for the ambulance – he simply stood and stared not knowing what to do for the best. These recollections intrude into the survivor's memory and regularly cause distress and associated strong emotional feelings.

☀ Recurrent and distressing dreams of the event

These dreams, like the recollections, must be recurrent and they must cause distress. They have been referred to earlier as 'night-terrors'. However, most people experience the occasional nightmare. A person who dreams of falling of a cliff and awakes in a cold sweat has simply had a bad dream. To qualify as a symptom of PTSD dreams should occur frequently and they should be linked directly to the trauma that has been suffered. The dreams may feature the whole traumatic event, or they might single out one or two aspects of the trauma which were particularly frightening.

☀ Suddenly acting or feeling as if the event were recurring (flashbacks)

The sudden acting out of the traumatic event as though it were happening all over again is usually referred to as a flashback. Flashbacks are extremely frightening for those who experience them and for those who witness the flashback.

The trauma victim may describe the flashback experience as 'having a video camera in their head'. The camera has a video tape of the trauma which suddenly starts running and the trauma is relived just as if it were happening all over again. For the survivor the problem centres on the fact they have no control over the play button on the video camera. The tape suddenly starts running and the survivor is thrown back into the trauma and it is all very real once again.

Furthermore, during a flashback the survivor loses the ability to distinguish between the past and the present as events merge into a single horrific trauma. Victims behave as though they are experiencing the original traumatic event and may be totally unaware of their behaviour and people around them. When the flashback subsides they will need a period of time to readjust to where they are. They will probably feel frightened and embarrassed and may even entertain the thought they may be 'going mad'. They will need sympathy and reassurance.

(*Note* – A recurrence of the trauma in the form of a flashback is far more involved than a straightforward recollection of the event although both will be distressing.)

●❋ *Intense psychological distress at exposure to cues of the event, phobias*

Traumatised people may develop fears and phobias about everyday objects and situations. They have quickly learned that particular sights, sounds, smells or situations will remind them of the trauma they experienced. This knowledge creates a sense of fear, anxiety, anger or impending doom when they come into contact with the cue which might trigger some sort of reminder of the event.

A child who witnessed a shooting may suddenly become frightened when he hears a car backfire or a door slam shut. This fright might make him disinclined to go outside where he might be subjected to sudden noises and a form of agoraphobia may develop. Another child who was abused while camping might develop a quite irrational fear of the sight of camping gas cylinders, or caravans, both being reminders of the location where she was abused.

Being unable to face certain situations or continue with the ordinary course of daily activities because of the possibility of reminders or re-exposure is a major feature of PTSD (Yule and Gold 1993, Kinchin 1992).

●❋ *Physiological reactivity on exposure to cues of the event*

Physiological reactivity might be described thus: a child is taking part in a life-saving course at the local swimming pool. All is proceeding according to plan until the instructor suggests getting into the water wearing clothes to simulate real-life situations. For the child who survived the capsizing of the *Herald of Free Enterprise* this mirrors the trauma she experienced and she may start to react to this reminder. The trigger or cue for this child was not swimming, it was wearing wet clothing. The child responds as if she were back on the capsizing ferry. She clambers as high as she can to get away from the water and studies the roof over the swimming pool as if seeking out a rescue helicopter.

This scenario discusses an extreme reaction. However, as we have seen earlier in this book, children who suffered during the sinking of the *Jupiter* cruise ship found it difficult to stand on the balcony of the school hall because it resembled the sloping decks of the ship. They did not imagine themselves back on the ship, but the distressing memory brought about by the similarity of the situation made them breathe irregularly, feel lightheaded, knotted their stomachs and caused other related symptoms which could be described succinctly as a panic attack.

Triggers for panic attacks can vary greatly. The stimuli may involve aspects such as smell, sound, texture, or a trick of the light. The list of potential triggers is as long as the list of potential traumas. For a child standing in a crowded lift this may be a reminder of a playground bullying incident. Smells in the school chemistry laboratory may remind a child of a motoring accident in which a car overturned and battery acid was spilled onto the hot engine. The stabbing of Caesar in a school Shakespearean production might bring back memories of a mugging which was witnessed by a child. Some reactions to situations will take the victim completely by surprise, adding to the distress brought about by the reactivation of the traumatic memory.

💣 Efforts to avoid thoughts, feelings, activities, places or people associated with the event

It is logical for people who have been traumatised to protect themselves from situations which may prolong the traumatic memory. In order to do this, they may intentionally avoid thoughts or feelings, and make concerted efforts to avoid activities or situations, that might trigger any recollection of the event.

This avoidance might focus on everyday activities such as refusing to get into a car (but being quite happy to travel by bus). It could be a refusal to attend school, or to attend certain lessons while at school, or perhaps a refusal to stand in the dinner queue or attend assembly because of the crowded atmosphere.

On one level, the refusal to discuss an event can be seen as avoidance. This is not a stubborn refusal to talk (which might be the case in other circumstances) but an agitated, and distressed refusal. (A genuine inability to remember should not be considered a refusal to talk.) Avoidance strategies might be obvious such as the use of alcohol or drugs to 'cloud' the traumatic memory. Overwork is sometimes used as a strategy to avoid thoughts and feelings about the trauma and although this behaviour might more usually be attributed to adults, it is not uncommon in adolescents and young adults.

Sometimes the survivor is very aware of the strategy being employed, but at other times they are totally unaware of the reason behind particular actions other than the knowledge that to proceed would be distressing and frightening.

💣 Inability to recall an important aspect of the event

It is common for people who suffer head injuries, or 'blackouts' (which may or may not be the consequence of alcohol or drug abuse), to be unable to remember events or to have a memory failure. Lack of ability to recall the event is not part of the criterion for PTSD in this context.

The 'psychogenic amnesia' which is reported by traumatised people is an inability to recall particular aspects of the trauma or its immediate aftermath. John LeCarré explains this wonderfully in his novel *Tinker, Tailor, Soldier, Spy*. He writes,

> There are moments which are made up of too much stuff for them to be lived at the time they occur.

During a traumatic incident a person's senses are working overtime. Sight, sound, smell, taste and touch are all channelling information as fast as they can and the victim's brain is trying to cope with this. It is quite natural, therefore, that some of the information is not assimilated and stored in the memory. A child who survives a road accident in which his mother is killed might not remember being told that 'Mummy is dead'. A girl who is being assaulted at knife point might not hear the sirens of the police car coming to her assistance and she might not recognise police officers – despite their uniform.

Jessica's story. I could see the knife glinting in the light. I could smell the aftershave of my attacker, but I couldn't hear what he was saying to me. His mouth was moving but I could not hear the words. It was as much a shock to me when the police car screeched to a stop beside us. I hadn't heard it coming.

There is so much going on during the trauma that it is impossible to memorise everything. There wasn't time for this to happen. Anecdotally, it is memories related to sounds which are most often missing.

💣 *Markedly diminished interest in significant activities*

The essential feature of this symptom is a lowering of interest in previously enjoyed events. However, for the symptom to occur the activities which are no longer of interest must have been very significant to the survivor prior to the trauma. The diminishing interest must not be part of what would otherwise be considered a normal developmental change.

Alan's story. Mum wanted to take me Christmas shopping. She wanted my advice about what to buy my brother and sister. I went along with her because I could see she was only trying to help. I could not face telling her that I didn't give a damn about Christmas.

A boy who was keen on football and a regular player in the school team would not usually be expected to stop playing football immediately after a boating accident. A girl who could not keep her nose out of books, prior to a trauma, would not generally be expected to ignore the written word in favour of idly watching television following the death of her baby brother. In both of these stereotypical examples the victim has abandoned an activity which was a part of their previous life – not just a passing interest.

In some cases avoidance might almost be seen as the survivor punishing themselves, by abstaining from something they previously relished. It is a way of coming to terms with their trauma and survival.

💣 *Feelings of detachment*

Once again, the essence of this symptom is that a person's character has changed after the trauma. If they were described as a 'bit of a loner' prior to the trauma then it might be difficult to apply this description following a traumatic incident. Some children prefer their own company.

A child from a family with a strong religious background might find that going to church after the death of her brother ceased to have meaning. She might feel alone and alienated, receiving no comfort and perceiving that her faith has betrayed her. She now attends church out of habit alone. This behaviour would not have been normal for her prior to the trauma.

The same might also apply to a teenager who attended a youth club and valued the support and friendship of the club and its leaders. However, following the witnessing of a serious car accident, she no longer entered into the spirit of the club, but just sat in the corner drinking coffee and smoking cigarettes. She no longer sought out her friends or the youth leader with whom she previously had a very strong (but totally appropriate) friendship.

In short, survivors switch off from, and maybe reject, their previous social groups.

💣 *Sense of a foreshortened future*

If a person has experienced a serious threat to their life, and they have almost been killed, they may suddenly become very aware that life is fragile and limited. Therefore, some trauma victims may not expect to have a career, or a marriage or children of their own. They are no longer surprised by the thought that they might not live to old age. They are not likely to engage in saving for future events, or pension plans.

This is not the same as a person who has no regard for their actions and becomes amoral as a consequence and says, 'So what if I get arrested – who cares?' That is not a sense of foreshortened future. That is an irresponsible attitude.

💣 *Sleep difficulties*

Sleep difficulties are divided into two groups: those people who have trouble falling asleep, and those who have difficulty staying asleep. If sleep is going to produce nightmares then many survivors will not want to fall asleep since that is a way of preventing the frightening dreams from happening.

Children often regress in sleep patterns, wanting to sleep with a light on, or in a room with someone else, or even in bed with their parents. Clock-watching, or appearing to be awake all night and watching the clock tick slowly round, but actually benefiting from a series of short naps, is actually quite common. However, this is often reported as very poor quality sleep and people who clock-watch are often tired during the day. (See Figure 3.1.)

> *Amy-Claire's story.* I was very bad tempered. I was always wide awake, even at four o'clock in the morning. I blamed everything on being too tired to cope. Mum and Dad even bought me a new bed.

Occasionally, this symptom is reversed and survivors have no difficulty sleeping – the problem becomes managing to stay awake. It is possible that constant sleeping could be a form of avoidance behaviour.

💣 *Irritability or outbursts of anger*

It is not surprising that PTSD survivors experience periods of general irritability and are at risk of suddenly losing their tempers over trivial matters. There is an awareness of the loss of control during angry outbursts which may be similar to any loss of control during the original trauma. Following such an outburst there is often a period of embarrassment and apology. (See Figure 3.2.)

TICK
TOCK
TICK
TOCK
TOCK
TICK
TOCK
TOCK
TICK
TICK
TOCK
TICK
TICK
TICK
TOCK
TICK
1 2 3 4 5 6 7 8 9 10 11

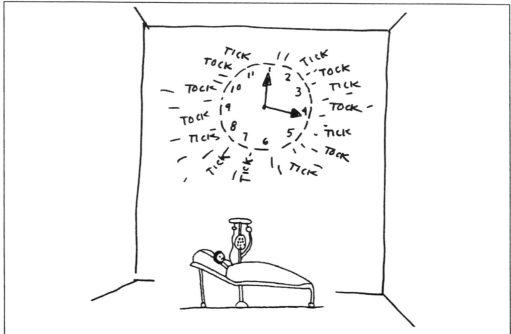

Terry describes how slowly the time passes while she lies in bed recovering after an accident. She says the 'drips' in her intravenous drip and the ticks of the clock make her head go mad.

Figure 3.1

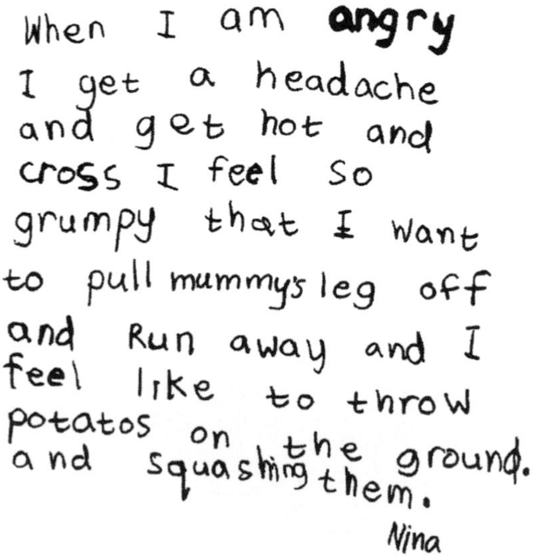

When I am angry
I get a headache
and get hot and
cross I feel So
grumpy that I want
to pull mummys leg off
and Run away and I
feel like to throw
potatos on the ground.
and squashing them.
Nina

Nina, age six, describes her strong feelings of anger – she says the fire could have been avoided.

Figure 3.2

☀ *Difficulty concentrating and remembering*

Trauma survivors frequently report great difficulty concentrating when they attempt simple tasks. Students asked to concentrate on classroom teaching, or on computations or reading, may find great difficulty in applying themselves to the task. This may partly be due to the intrusive images which occupy their thoughts.

Survivors may also experience difficulties remembering details such as their mobile phone number or e-mail address. They may forget the route home from school, or which lesson timetable they should be following. Circumstances which can be explained as simple absent-mindedness in older people is extremely frustrating and vexing to child survivors.

> *Anne's story.* Detention! All I had done was forgotten which books to bring to the lesson. Why couldn't she understand that? I didn't do it deliberately. I just threw my bag across the room and stamped out. Tears – I cried for ages. Nobody found me. I escaped from school and wandered around the town.

☀ *Hypervigilance*

A child who has been mugged will pay excessive attention to what is going on around him. This is not a general suspiciousness of situations. It is a detailed and persistent search for any clues which might alert the survivor to further trouble of any description.

Survivors will often study people if they are within close proximity. They are seeking out potential dangers. Survivors may well stand with their backs to walls to limit the number of directions from which potential dangers can arrive. The level of vigilance is 'hyper', that is, far beyond that required from a realistic appraisal of the situation.

☀ *Exaggerated startle response*

Survivors may be disturbed by any sudden noise or movement. In this case the individual may exhibit a startle response which is totally disproportionate to both the stimulus and behaviour which would normally be expected in such circumstances.

> *Darren's story.* He asked for it. He tapped me on the shoulder – I didn't know he was there. I was so angry I just hit out. I didn't mean to make his nose bleed. He just didn't understand – like the rest didn't.

☀ *Developmental regression*

Young children may regress developmentally following a trauma. Anecdotal evidence suggests that this regression might be by as much as two to three years and may be observed by the way a child plays, eats, sleeps or seeks attention. Thumb-sucking, baby talk, drinking from a bottle, returning to the support of a previously discarded 'cuddly' toy and bedwetting are the most obvious signs that a young child's development is in temporary regression (Scott and Palmer 2000). Recently acquired skills may become lost and children may show clinging behaviour, not wanting to leave a parent in the mornings and not wanting to leave school at the end of the day (Brown 1999).

(*Note* – All of these behaviours (clinging, thumb-sucking, etc.) are normal behaviours and should only be considered as symptoms of PTSD if the child regresses to this behaviour, having previously outgrown it.)

☀ Physical pains

Many survivors may appear to be suffering from physical injuries. Although not physically hurt they may experience back pains, muscle cramps or severe headaches. The causes of these pains will probably be psychosomatic, but the actual pain they feel is real and may require treatment in its own right.

Connor's story. By the end of the day I couldn't stand up and walk. My legs just wouldn't work properly. I thought I was going mad because there was nothing wrong with my legs. It was the doctor who explained, to Mum on the phone, that it was just muscle cramps. My legs hurt – I wanted to walk so badly.

☀ Depression

Adolescent survivors commonly report significantly high rates of depression (Yule 1999). They may have strong suicidal thoughts and take overdoses in the year after the trauma. A significant number become very anxious after accidents.

In the light of the other symptoms, feelings of depression and anxiety should be expected and anticipated. Life has changed and the future no longer looks rosy.

Treatments

Specialists should administer most treatments for PTSD. Doctors, therapists and counsellors with expertise will be required in many cases. There is much debate about whether the symptoms should be treated or the memory of the trauma addressed. In practice, the treatment required is a blend of both factors.

Many children and adolescents will require medication at various stages of their recovery. They may need help sleeping, or relaxing or with pain relief. They might also need intervention by a specialist therapist at significant stages in their recovery. Most importantly, they need people to listen to them and to show understanding of their traumatic memory.

Control

Experience has suggested that the need of the majority of traumatised adults is to regain control of their lives (Kinchin 1998). This will include regaining control of the traumatic memory, and the procedures and interventions used to reach that goal. Children are no different in this respect. They will want to talk about their experiences. Attempting to force a child's pace is, however, likely to prove counter-productive. Nevertheless, it is good to encourage children to communicate since talking about the event will help recovery. This needs to be balanced against the risk of forcing the issue for children who are not ready to talk (Brown 1999).

Short-, medium-, long-term views of treatment

In the short term, after the immediate aftermath of a traumatic incident, people suffer post-traumatic stress rather than PTSD. In the adult world this is the time when many psychologists will be advocating the use of CID (Critical Incident Debriefing) as a method of reducing the traumatic memory (Hambling 1997).

Debriefing

Much has been written about CID or CISD (Critical Incident Stress Debriefing (Yule and Canterbury 1994)) or PD (Psychological Debriefing (Robinson and Mitchell 1993)) and the authors of this book do not wish to enter into the debate here.

Various methods have been adopted since 1983 and tried with considerable success. Conversely, however, there is a school of thought which suggests that CID makes people worse – not better. Perhaps the only conclusion that can be drawn is that CID is a very contentious issue (Rose 2000). Debriefing frequently looks at the trauma under three headings, namely: Facts, Feelings and Future. Using this 3Fs approach it is possible to work through the trauma in some considerable detail.

An alternative to CID is ISCI (Incident Specific Crisis Intervention) which is currently practised by Elizabeth Capewell at the Centre for Crisis Management and Education, Newbury. Capewell advocates that this type of intervention should be tailored to suit individual events. Appropriate intervention will depend upon the dynamics of the group, the incident, the context of the event and the extent to which ISCI is possible. ISCI is a form of debriefing which acts as a base from which other treatments may emerge. If CID is the chosen path it is essential to ensure the persons leading the debriefing (there should always be at least two) are suitably qualified for the task. Debriefing is not counselling. It is quite specifically a debriefing for all those who were involved in the incident and it may be applied to groups or individuals. Debriefing is *not* a cure or treatment for PTSD, neither is it a way of safeguarding people against PTSD. Rather, CID *may* reduce the risk of victims subsequently being diagnosed as suffering from PTSD, particularly when the intervention occurs soon after the event.

In the medium term (more than one month after the traumatic incident) victims can be formally diagnosed as suffering from PTSD. Ironically, this is also the time when those around the victim may start to relax their vigilance and start to feel that the trauma has not manifest any serious consequences. If the survivor has managed to adopt excellent avoidance strategies and been able to cover up the other symptoms of the disorder then it may be quite easy for the underlying disorder to go totally undetected for a month or more. After that time, the strain will start to take its toll, the symptoms will start to break through, and cracks will appear in the coping veneer.

Chronic PTSD

In the long term, PTSD survivors may experience further problems. If PTSD has gone undetected for six months then a person's behaviour patterns have almost certainly become well established and the symptoms will be difficult to relieve. Thus long-term or chronic PTSD is much more difficult to treat and to diagnose because it is not always obvious which traumatic incident triggered the disorder. Children who have been abused in any way might well fall into the category of chronic PTSD survivors and it may take some considerable time to establish precisely what the traumatic events are and how the memory of the trauma is affecting the child. Abuse is considered in Chapter 4.

Play therapy, Art therapy

Many schools provide facilities for a variety of play and art therapists to operate, without having to 'take the child out of school'. This therapy (for more detail see Dwivedi (2000)) offers children a non-verbal, symbolic language, through which to tell their story and express themselves. Indeed, therapy should be encouraged with PTSD victims as a way of allowing them to mix with other children and to rebuild their self-esteem.

Adult victims have affirmed the positive effect achieved by alternative therapies. Although not generally recognised treatments, there are good practitioners whose work has been highly regarded.

Natalie's story. The children jumped on my bed in the mornings and shook me to wake up and play with them. I have nine sisters and all of their babies know me well now and run towards me when I call round. I have been very fortunate indeed. Baby therapy has been fantastic. Children cannot hurt you and if you love them and are left in charge of them, how can you possibly ruminate about your problem?

The benefits of different therapies are commended by many victims of PTSD. If children are suffering from PTSD then mixing with younger children or infants may prove beneficial. Natalie affirms the benefits for adults too.

In addition to these therapies, animals can help provide comfort and support. Many children's hospices use domestic pets, or bigger animals, encouraging children to handle the animals, and to communicate their feelings.

Listening

The development of listening skills is important so that effective listening can be offered to those who want to talk about their problem. However, in order to provide high standards of support it is important for carers to develop their listening capacities.

Eye-Movement Desensitisation Reprocessing

A system of treatment devised in the USA during the late 1980s is Eye-Movement Desensitisation and Reprocessing (EMDR). The introduction of EMDR by Dr Francine Shapiro in 1978, was greeted with excitement mixed with controversy. The process involves talking about the traumatic memory while focusing on the rapidly moving finger of the therapist. The moving finger induces what is described as saccadic eye movements similar to the movements the eye makes when someone is in deep sleep and dreaming. By focusing on the finger and concentrating on the traumatic memory the severity of the trauma is dramatically reduced. There are a number of very reliable studies which support EMDR as a treatment (Puffer *et al.* 1998).

Like all new treatments it is essential that the benefits are validated and accepted by both therapists and their patients. It has been suggested by some researchers (Scott and Palmer 2000) that EMDR is very similar to the eighteenth-century cure of Mesmerism – a psychosocial intervention promoted by the Austrian physician Mesmer. Scott and Palmer advocate that well-established 'safe' cures are more likely to serve survivors' needs in the new millennium.

Summary

It is important to note that PTSD is always treatable. Indeed, full recovery should be the predicted outcome for each individual. However, many young people will demonstrate changed behaviour during this period of adjustment (see Table 3.1). The meaning of full recovery is discussed in Chapter eight.

Table 3.1 Changes in behaviour

Pre-school children	Primary-age children	Adolescents
• withdrawn • lethargic • non-communicative • regressive behaviour • role play and re-enactment of trauma • increased dependency on adults	• regression in school performance • concentration difficulties • physical and psychosomatic symptoms • sleep disorders • immature behaviour • aggressive • school refusal • withdrawn and clinging • incontinence • night terrors • re-enactment of the incident	• depression • suicidal tendencies • hypervigilance • anxiety • survivor guilt • inappropriate sexual behaviour • truancy • substance abuse • sleep disturbance • decline in academic attainment

CHAPTER 4

The trauma of abuse

> Every abused child is in some way victimised, but not every abused child is traumatised. Working with children who have been traumatised requires an understanding of the potential impact on the developing child. (Schofield 1997)

Child abuse is typically described as physical, emotional or sexual. The wording 'significant harm' in the Children Act 1989 has resulted in a shift away from determining the circumstances of abuse to ascertaining the effect of maltreatment or neglect on the child.

Abuse transcends all cultural, religious or social settings and although a child may experience all manner of abuse, one type is usually dominant within the child's life. Surveys conducted in Great Britain and the United States suggest approximately one in every ten children has suffered abuse (Mallon 1997) and that 13 per cent of women and 8 per cent of men have experienced some form of abuse by the time they are 18 years of age (NCH Action for Children 1995).

The trauma of abuse has long-lasting effects on children, with some researchers concluding sexual abuse causes the greatest damage (Draijer 1994). If sexual abuse is combined with other abuse the effects are potentially extremely damaging. We believe the severity of the abuse is a significant factor in determining the harm done to individual children. However we also acknowledge many children suffer more than one form of maltreatment or neglect and it is often the accumulation of this that causes long-term harm.

Abused children frequently demonstrate behaviour associated with PTSD which can overwhelm their coping responses. Schofield (1997) describes two levels of trauma response with different characteristics. The first type involves a single event and the child recalling in detail what happened. The second type concerns long-standing situations of maltreatment or abuse where the child may develop coping strategies. In these circumstances the child attempts to deny the event and they may create 'a day-time self' and 'a night-time self'.

The abuse category under which a child is registered as abused is a matter for professional judgement. However the definitions of abuse are those set out in the Children Act 1989 (para. 6 sub-point 40). An abuser is someone who aims at using the child as a means of his or her own satisfaction without regard for the child's wishes. Often the abuser will be in a care-taking position; be aware that what is happening is taboo; exert power over the child; deceive the child into believing what is happening is a result of the child's encouragement or behaviour; be aware of the child's fear.

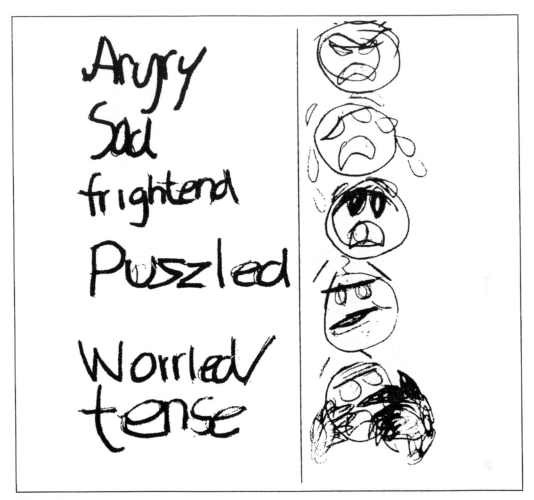

Figure 4.1

Neglect

Neglect is considered to be present if there is failure to protect the child from exposure to any kind of danger, including cold and starvation, or extreme failure to carry out important aspects of care, which result in significant impairment of the child's health or development. This includes non-organic failure to thrive. A child's health and well-being is often determined by the quality of family life and the parenting that he or she receives. Parenting that is 'low on warmth and high on criticism' is known to be harmful (Thoburn *et al.* 1995).

Many children are under threat of neglect, not through wilful negligence of their parents but as a result of poverty or unemployment. Others may not be directly abused themselves but they may be traumatised as they grow up in an environment where they witness domestic violence between adults.

Indicators of neglect

Possible indicators of neglect include:

- constant hunger;
- poor personal hygiene;
- constant tiredness;
- poor state of clothing;
- emaciation;
- frequent lateness or non-attendance at school;
- untreated medical problems;
- destructive tendencies;
- low self-esteem;
- behaviour such as rocking, thumb-sucking, hair-twisting;
- running away;
- scavenging for food or clothes.

Physical abuse

Physical abuse is considered to be present if there is actual or likely physical injury to a child, or failure to prevent physical injury (or suffering).

My moth falls down when I'm not sewre

Figure 4.2

Indicators of physical abuse

Possible indicators of physical abuse include:

- unexplained injuries or burns;
- improbable explanations for injuries;
- refusal to discuss injuries;
- untreated injuries;
- fear of parents being contacted;
- withdrawal from physical contact;
- arriving at school early/fear of returning home;
- fear of medical help;
- self-destructive tendencies;
- aggression towards others;
- running away.

At a recent professional development day, teachers described behaviours in their pupils (see Figure 4.3).

truancy
stealing
depression
over-eating
under-eating
glue sniffing
self-mutilation
low self-esteem
suicide attempts
dirty appearance
sleep disturbances
drug/alcohol abuse
physical abuse signs
unkempt appearance
chronic running away
isolation from friends
first to arrive at school
inability to concentrate
refusal to speak in class
promiscuous behaviour
pseudo-mature behaviour
last to depart from school
unusual fear of going home
overly compliant behaviour
attention-seeking behaviour
frequent lateness or absence
sudden drop in achievement
repeated physical complaints
tiredness, lethargy, listlessness
refusal to undress for PE/games
withdrawal from social activities
persistent sexual play with peers
inappropriate seductive behaviour
compulsive need to excel at school
non-participation in school social activities
extreme fear of being left alone with adults
unusually heavy household or child-care duties

Figure 4.3 Behaviours in pupils

Sexual abuse

Although there are many circumstances in which sexual abuse occurs, the term relates to actual or likely exploitation of a child or adolescent. The degree of harm caused by sexual abuse depends on factors such as the age of the child, the relationship with the perpetrator and the intensity and duration of the abuse. According to Gordon (1989) premeditated planned incest that is calculated to avoid chance of the perpetrator being caught, is widespread. Furthermore Kroth (1988) believes uninvolved siblings in families where incest occurs may be at risk of distress. There is a growing body of evidence that suggests that many child sexual abusers are children or young people themselves, often under the age of 18 (Fahrenback *et al.* 1986, National Children's Home 1992).

Abuse during very early childhood affects the child's psychological development and may result in poor self-esteem. In adolescence the sexuality of the young person may be severely affected and this often results in the young person experiencing difficulty in forming relationships with other people. The findings of several investigations indicate that a significant proportion of children who are sexually abused suffer many symptoms of Post-Traumatic Stress Disorder (Deblinger *et al.* 1996).

How adults respond when a child discloses they are a victim of sexual abuse plays a crucial part in the child's future development. Above all children need to know they will be believed and protected. Mallon (1997) believes some children rely on adults to 'lend' them power until the crisis is over.

Indicators of sexual abuse
Possible indicators include:

- disclosure by the child or hints about secrets they cannot tell;
- personality changes, such as clinging behaviour or withdrawal;
- aggressive behaviour or temper tantrums;
- regression to younger behaviour with incontinence, thumb-sucking, etc.;
- sexually explicit behaviour which is inappropriate to the child's age;
- inappropriate sexual play;
- inability to concentrate;
- hypervigilance;
- night terrors;
- urinary infections, soreness or bleeding in the genital area;
- changed eating patterns;
- chronic physical ailments such as stomach-ache or headache;
- poor self-image or self-mutilation;
- reluctance to go to the place where the abuse is occurring;
- running away from home;
- relationships with adults who are secretive and exclude others.

(Based on NSPCC 1995)

Emotional abuse and bullying

Emotional abuse includes actual (or likely) adverse effects on the child's emotional and behavioural development caused by persistent or severe emotional ill-treatment or rejection. Typically children who are abused by their parents encounter a lack of care and warmth.

There are many definitions of bullying, but most have three common elements:

- the behaviour is deliberately harmful;
- the behaviour is repeated over a period of time;
- the victim has difficulty defending themselves.

(Marr and Field 2001)

Indicators of emotional abuse
Possible indicators of emotional abuse will include:

- physical, mental and emotional delay;
- over-reaction to mistakes;
- sudden speech or communication disorders;
- fear of new situations;
- inappropriate emotional responses to painful situations;
- uncharacteristic behaviour such as thumb-sucking, hair-twisting or rocking;
- fear of parents being contacted;
- extremes of passivity or aggression;
- running away;
- drug or solvent abuse;
- compulsive stealing;
- scavenging for food or clothes.

Furness (1991) writes of secondary damage and traumatisation that can result if support for children is uncoordinated. Indeed, a Department of Health Report (1991) warns professionals to take great care when planning intervention, since parents who are involved in investigations of child abuse will normally feel threatened (Cleaver and Freeman 1995).

The balance needs to be struck between taking action designed to protect the child from abuse whilst at the same time protecting him or her and the family from the harm caused by the unnecessary intervention. (p. 27)

Separation

Many children who are abused are separated from their families as a result of child protection procedures, legal decisions or because their parents are unable to cope. Whatever the circumstances of the separation, the child will have experienced profound loss. The effects of separation are described elsewhere in the book, but in the context of this chapter it seems pertinent to note that when children experience stress they turn to an attachment figure, for help and comfort. If the cause of the child's stress is the attachment figure they may not know where to seek solace. According to Fahlberg (1984) young children may even perceive they have been kidnapped or given away if they are taken into care. Their confidence and security is threatened and many will believe they were in some way responsible for what happened. Sometimes children are separated from all the members of their family and they live in unfamiliar surroundings. Thus, in addition to the abuse, they have to adapt to changes in their care. Aldgate and Simmonds (1988) describe the symptoms of trauma in children as very like those of bereavement.

Amy's story. First my new Dad touched me where he shouldn't. I told my Mum and she told our social worker. Then I got sent away into a care place. I wish I hadn't told my Mum because then she wouldn't still be with the new Dad and I wouldn't be in care.

How can adults help?

- Understand the nature of the abuse and the likely harm to the child, as a result of the abuse.
- Take into account the effects of all the losses experienced by the child or adolescent, not just the abuse.
- Take into account the child's physical, emotional and cognitive development.
- Take into account the context in which the child is being cared.
- Take into account religious and cultural needs.
- Take into account important people in the child's life.

Summary

Childhood sexual abuse is a well-known high risk factor for development of PTSD in adults and there is a vast amount of literature on the effects of childhood sexual abuse on adults. It has, however, only very recently been acknowledged that children can suffer PTSD symptoms, as its immediate after-effects (Pandit and Shah 2000).

It is estimated approximately one in every ten children has suffered abuse. The Children Act 1989 outlined the categories of abuse. In more recent years there has been a move away from determining the circumstances of abuse to ascertaining the effects of maltreatment or neglect on the child.

Many children who are the victims of abuse are separated from their families as the result of child protection procedures, legal decisions or because their parents are unable to care for them. Thus, in addition to the abuse, they have to adapt to unfamiliar surroundings and to new people. The trauma has long-lasting effects on children and they frequently demonstrate behaviour associated with PTSD

CHAPTER 5

The trauma of bereavement

Just as children form relationships and attachments, so they lose them and these losses may be incredibly difficult to come to terms with. Through the process of attachment, the child develops a sense of identity as a person who is loveable and who can function in competent, responsible ways in relationships with other people, and with the world around. Loss threatens these foundations and undermines feelings of healthy self-esteem. When loss of self-esteem is compounded by self-blame, confusion and grief, a child's well-being may be severely at risk. Furthermore if children are denied the right to take some control over their lives their self-esteem may deteriorate even further and give rise to feelings of anxiety, confusion and anger. Adjusting to bereavement is often described as a series of orderly stages, yet both adults and children may experience a myriad of emotional responses that will be particular to individuals. Hodgkinson and Stewart (1991) are of the opinion that there is no empirical evidence to suggest that stages exist and that a much more useful approach to understanding grief is an acceptance that people experience a number of interrelated thoughts, feelings and behaviours.

Untimely death

Although bereavement is a universal phenomenon Raphael (1986) believes that about a third of people experiencing major bereavements have a poor outcome in terms of resolution. Sudden, untimely or unexpected deaths or those that are horrific represent highest risk (Brown 1999). (See Figure 5.1.)

There are three major types of untimely death: premature death, unexpected death and calamitous death. Premature death such as the death of a sibling or peer jeopardises emotional reality and faith in an investment for the future. Calamitous deaths, because they are often violent and destructive, may shake a child's emotional investment in the predictable order and pattern of daily life, and the sudden, unexpected bereavement may result in disbelief and severe shock. Children's responses to untimely death differ from adults' in several ways. Developmentally children are less well equipped to cope with loss and depending on their age and aptitude their experience and cognitive skills are likely to be limited and their capacity to make sense of what has happened is subsequently reduced. They also have less control over their circumstances and their environment than adults and they are dependent on others to recognise their grief and to fulfil and anticipate their needs.

'When the bus crashed they all fell down dead' –
brother, aged 3, of M40 minibus disaster victim.

Figure 5.1

Disenfranchised grief

Doka (1993) speaks of disenfranchised grief in children who may feel disempowered in their emotional expression of significant losses in their lives. This is largely because other people do not acknowledge their need to mourn. He argues that in part disenfranchised grief is born out of the long-held assumption that children do not fully experience the impact or permanence of death until adolescence.

Cindy's Story: Cindy's parents separated before she was born and divorced when she was six months old. Her mother and maternal grandparents brought her up. When Cindy was 11 her father died of a heart attack and she became withdrawn and developed an eating disorder. Cindy grieved for the relationship she had never had in the past and could never dream of in the future.

Complicated mourning

Complicated mourning has three main elements:

- Symptoms – which may be psychological, behavioural, social or physical.
- Syndromes – which may be independent of each other or combined to create complicated mourning symptoms. Syndromes include: delayed mourning; chronic mourning; inhibited mourning.
- Mental or physical disorders – these disorders were described by the American Psychiatric Association for PTSD and are detailed in Chapter 1.

There are several factors that may potentially complicate mourning:

- diminished coping capacities as a result of shock;
- a sense of heightened vulnerability with loss of security and self-confidence;
- realisation of a non-orderly unpredictable world;
- senselessness of the event;
- unfinished business with no chance to say 'goodbye';
- attempt to reconstruct the sequence of events in order to comprehend what happened;
- determination to blame or affix responsibility for the death;
- secondary losses, for example loss of a home or financial security;
- intrusion of traumatic memories (PTSD).

(Brown 1999)

Violent or traumatic death

Traumatic death has been described as an emotional state of discomfort and stress resulting from an extraordinary catastrophic experience that shatters the survivor's sense of safety. While any death may be potentially traumatic for survivors, there are circumstances of death that are especially traumatic.

Violent deaths are particularly traumatic because of the frightening and vulnerable feelings they create in survivors. Rynearson (1987) believes that violent death is particularly associated with Post-Traumatic Stress Disorder.

Matthew, aged 3½, remembers the night his daddy killed his mummy. He says his eyebrows 'jumped off'.

Figure 5.2

Many survivors of violent death experience imagery of the event for long periods afterwards. This interferes with their mourning. Children may recall past thoughts where they perhaps wished the person harm and this in turn leads to feelings of guilt and shame that they were in some way to blame. Where murder is the cause of violent death, Redmond (1989) believes that the likelihood of Post-Traumatic Stress Disorder is even greater.

Multiple death

Situations that involve multiple deaths can be particularly traumatic for children and result in what Kastenbaum (1969) calls 'bereavement overload'. In the context of traumatic death multiple deaths include accidents, natural disasters or multiple murder scenarios.

Children not only suffer the trauma of the bereavement but in some instances they mourn for more than one person to whom they have an attachment. Thus their grief becomes a vicious cycle of incomplete mourning that includes:

- trying to prioritise the order of mourning (for more than one person);
- struggling to differentiate emotional attachments held for the persons who have died;
- loss of security;
- an overwhelming terror of the event;
- a sense of survivor guilt.

(Brown 1999)

Personal encounter with death

Where a child experiences a situation in which there is a significant threat to survival or a shocking confrontation with the death of other persons, this may result in intense psychological reactions. Raphael (1986) writes that intrusive repetitive images are extremely common where there has been a threat to life and an individual is rendered helpless. Children frequently speak of what they did or were unable to do in order to survive. Children's emotional responses may include:

- fear of abandonment;
- anxiety about the future;
- a sense of being out of control;
- yearning for a return to normal patterns of life;
- psychosomatic responses, for example sickness, tummy ache, joint pains.

As with other types of trauma there is often a need for children to attempt to shut out or deny the event. Alternatively they may confront the memory of the experience in an attempt to make sense of what happened.

It is important to note that PTSD is not always the result of a personal threat to self or witnessing the death of others. We have worked with children who have been unprepared for a visit to a chapel of rest to view the body of someone close to them. These children have shown many of the responses already discussed. Where very young children have been unprepared they often communicate a heightened awareness of sensory perceptions when they saw the body, for example coldness of skin, smell of the room (or sometimes flowers or candles), the sight of a head and perhaps hands, but no other part of the body. Encounters with sensory stimuli afterwards have triggered intrusive images and nightmares similar to the original situation.

Sudden death

Sudden and unexpected death may affect the child's coping strategies so adversely that a traumatic experience is suffered, even though the circumstances of the death may not be traumatic. Raphael (1986) refers to this as the 'shock effect' of sudden death. With no time to anticipate the loss, the child experiences an overwhelming and over-powering emotional response, leaving him feeling confused, out of control and unable to grasp the full implications of the loss. Quite simply he is in shock emotionally and psychologically, which prevents his capacity to grasp what has happened and exacerbates the intensity of his grief. (See Figure 5.3.)

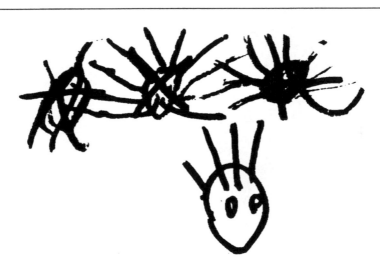

Rob describes how the news of the car accident made him very frightened. His hair 'prickles', he says, when he thinks about what happened.

Figure 5.3

Preventable death

Preventable death presents child survivors with many complications that may increase the duration and severity of their grief (Bugen 1979). Anger may be intensified and the preventability of the situation may result in children spending vast amounts of time and emotional energy, searching for a reason or cause so that a determinant for blame may be found. Children often describe violent thoughts directed at the perceived cause of death and the violation of the child's assumptive secure world makes it very difficult for him to make any sense out of the event or to protect himself in the future. Sometimes children attach blame for what has happened to themselves because it is easier to cope with the event being their responsibility and potentially being within their control.

The trauma of family bereavement

Bereavement for children is influenced by many factors including their age, level of cognitive understanding and the relationship that they had with the person who died. These factors will influence the child's emotional and behavioural responses. Separation has a powerful effect on young babies and as children grow older the effects become more complex. This not only applies to children; separation from a person who is needed for whatever reason may cause anxiety in adults. As babies we learn that if we protest about our separation, an adult will come and comfort us. This lays the foundation for understanding that comfort is attainable through our actions and our emotional responses. Gradually young children learn to cope with separation and come to understand that changes as well as disappearances are reversible. But when life experiences prove that some losses (such as those through death) are permanent, high levels of anxiety may be attached to separation (Brown 1999).

There is evidence (for example Herbert 1991, Parkes 1983) that working with a family is the most effective way of helping bereaved children. However, most children have far less control and access to information than adults do. In the case of traumatic circumstances, a child may be bereft of family members. It is these areas of control and access which separate children's experience of death from that of the adults involved. Children adapting to grief need both cognitive and emotional understanding of what has happened. The starting point should be helping parents or primary carers to support the child in this process.

Parent with a terminal illness

Death is not in the scheme of things when you are a child. It is often premature and unexpected. It is an event that interferes with the normal process of growing up and plays on emotions which may never have been experienced before. In short, the death of a parent is shocking and the foundations of a child's life are rocked; their confidence in the world they know is destroyed.

Often children will describe their response to the news of terminal illness as one of helplessness and disbelief, which leaves them terrified, alone and anxious. Young children may make little sense of the situation and retreat, deny or explode, showing despair, or continue to behave as if nothing has happened. Their world is no longer a trusted place and bedwetting, thumb-sucking and nightmares are frequent expressions of emotional stress. Marked changes in behaviour such as mirroring the sick person may indicate stresses with which the child is ill equipped to cope.

Older children show a greater awareness of physical deterioration and of the dependency of the seriously ill adult. Where families are endeavouring to support a member who is life-threatened, allowing the young person to gain independence can become complicated. Indeed some adolescents may need permission to move on when the pressure to stay at home becomes too great.

Seventeen-year-old Janet recalls what it was like when her father became terminally ill.

I knew the treatment wasn't working and I'd suddenly find myself crying – on the bus; in the shower; at school. At night I used to go to my room and cry myself to sleep. I didn't cry in front of my sister and my Mum because they got so upset – it was as if a shroud of secrecy was wrapped around me. I spent all the evenings and weekends that winter at home in the house. I couldn't face the people who asked how Dad was and those who didn't bother to enquire. I remember on the day he died watching my mother and my grandparents and thinking how hard it was for them. It's two years since he died and I know I can never leave home now.

For a child whose parent is dying, the bewilderment and confusion may be both in the world around and within themselves. The long-term emotional difficulties may be considerable. Brown and Harris (1989) believe that the death of a parent before the age of 12 is likely to increase the chances of depressive reactions in adulthood.

In addition to the sorrow and loneliness experienced when a parent is dying, children may feel doubly abandoned by their surviving parent who is struggling to manage their own grief. Anger and guilt may also be part of children's feelings if they believe they were to blame for what happened. This is especially prevalent when there has been conflict or anger towards the person who is dying or with young children in a magical stage of conceptual thinking.

Many children will deny the reality of their parent's impending death because the experience and the long-term consequences are too painful to manage. Dyregrov (1991) describes this response as automatic emotional defence and he writes of children who on hearing the news turn to issues such as, 'Will I be able to use his bed after he has died?' or 'Can we start to plan for the funeral?'

Where children develop strategies like this it is not unusual for strong or violent feelings to emerge in other circumstances. Their reactions may then be out of proportion to the issue in hand.

Dominic was 11 when his father died after a long illness. He appeared to cope with the news in a very matter of fact way. However, the night before his funeral, his mother asked him to clean his shoes ready for the morning. He stormed out of the kitchen in a rage declaring 'I suppose the way I look is more important to you than all the times we didn't have to say good-bye.'

Black and Urbanowicz (1987), and Raphael (1986), have shown that over half a group of children studied suffered from long-term psychological problems for up to a year after the death of their parent. Two years later 30 per cent of the same young people were still experiencing adverse reactions, some of which might be described as pathological grief.

Tina was 14 the Christmas after her father was diagnosed with an incurable disease. On Christmas morning she stayed in bed for as long as she could and then told her mother she was going for a walk. When her mother reminded her it was Christmas Day she said

'I'm going out anyway because I don't see any point in sitting around pretending to be happy'. Later she returned home and cried in her mother's arms. This was the first time in eight months Tina had shown any grief.

Violent or sudden death of a parent

Bereavement is particularly hard when it is violent or sudden. The image left in children's minds may be debilitating and they may lose trust in the world. Small children may focus their play around the trauma. Bergen (1958) writes of a young child of four years who had watched one of her parents being murdered. She seized paints and a brush and, after painting the hands red, stabbed herself in the chest with a paintbrush.

Where death has occurred suddenly, some children will recall events which happened immediately before, examining conversations and their own relationship with the person in great detail. Abrams (1992) writes 'perhaps the hardest aspect of parent's death for young people – and the one most consistently overlooked and misunderstood – is that death, mourning and grief involve feelings of helplessness and a lack of control that are exceptionally difficult to cope with when you are at precisely the stage in your own life when you need to feel powerful and in control.'

Some children will need support or extra help and counselling after the death of a parent, especially if they show evidence of:

- preoccupation with death;
- changed behaviour (for example withdrawal);
- compulsive caregiving to siblings or adults;
- euphoria or putting the deceased person on a pedestal;
- accident proneness or psychosomatic illnesses;
- unwillingness to speak about the deceased person;
- lack of capacity to form new relationships.

(Brown 1999)

Telling children about an anticipated death

Information is essential if children are expected to cope with death realistically. Yet so often adults avoid the subject in the belief that children will cope better. This idea of 'ignorance is bliss' often leads to a concealment of the facts, especially if the death is anticipated. It may also deprive families from making the best use of the time which is left.

The effect of breaking bad news will inevitably cause immediate psychological injury to the child who hears it. Young people are acutely aware of the emotional responses of adults and adept at piecing together information. The best people to break bad news are adults who know the child well. The setting in which the information is given should be familiar, and where possible information should be as accurate as can be. For example, it is helpful to use the word 'dead' since euphemisms and metaphors are easily misconstrued, especially by young children who may be confused if they attempt to merge abstract and concrete concepts. If the death was expected and the child has been aware of this, then there will be a known context in which the event has happened. If not, children should be given some

facts, for example 'there has been a bad accident' or 'the sickness was just too much for ....
to carry on'.

How to break bad news

- Have someone the child knows break the news.
- Choose a familiar place.
- Give the information accurately, and if possible supported by facts about the context in which the death occurred.
- Use the words 'dead', 'died', etc.
- Allow uninterrupted time to sit with the child after the news has been given.
- Repeat the information.
- Allow the child to respond in any way they wish as long as they are not putting themselves at risk.
- Encourage children to ask questions.
- Reassure the child that someone will continue to care for them.
(Brown 1999)

Dyregrov (1991) says 'Adults have a tendency to exclude children when it comes to rituals.' But just like adults, children need to have the opportunity to say farewell and to participate in a ceremony, which will help them to make the unreal become real. However, there is some evidence to suggest involving children in rituals without adequate preparation may lead to trauma.

The decision whether a child should see a person after they have died must be a family one. Viewing a dead body is probably still the exception rather than the rule, but sometimes children express a deep desire to see the person after they have died; they may become bitter and enraged if they feel they are excluded. If a child wishes to pay a visit to the dead person, preparation beforehand is essential. This should include an explanation of how the dead person will look different from when they were alive. If adults have already visited the body, they will be able to give the child more information so that the context in which the visit takes place will be known. This helps to allay fears.

How can adults help?

- Allow the child to visit the dead person if they express a wish to do so.
- Prepare children carefully before the visit, explaining what to expect.
- Visit the body with a family member or someone who knows the child.
- Allow children to touch the body if they want.
- Encourage children to express whatever emotion they wish.
- Allow time to communicate or to 'play out' impressions of the visit afterwards.

Before the funeral

Before the funeral it is helpful if children can be given information. This might include describing the building in which the service will take place; how the coffin will be carried into the place and where it will be put; the people who will take part in the service and what they will do. For young children who have not developed abstract concepts, it will be helpful if they are able to participate in rituals, for example doing a drawing to be put in the coffin before the funeral or placing some flowers on the coffin at the funeral. Older children and adolescents should be encouraged to do what they feel is right. This may include spending some time alone with the deceased person before the funeral or taking an active role in the organisation or format of the service. Other youngsters may not wish to be active participants in the rituals immediately after the death or at the funeral. As a rule of thumb, adults should respect their wishes.

If the body of the person is to be cremated, it is particularly important that young children know that dead means not being able to move, eat, breathe, etc. Where children have had past experience of pets dying and have witnessed the burial of these, they may have an understanding of decay. They should be helped to understand that just as a body, which is dead and decayed, feels no sensations, so it is during cremation. For children from faith backgrounds this may be easier since they may be familiar with the idea of the body being a 'shell' which is left behind after the spirit has gone.

Children who need specialised professional support

There are occasions when the circumstances of death will almost inevitably cause a child to experience complicated grief. Generally it is not how the child is responding to the bereavement that is significant, but for how long. After several months have elapsed the child may be experiencing trauma if:

- they appear sad or depressed all the time;
- they are unable to relax or have not returned to activities which interested them before the bereavement;
- they lack self-esteem or express feelings of self-recrimination or worthlessness;
- they become persistently aggressive;
- they seem withdrawn;
- they are suffering from bouts of physical illness;
- they are perpetually tired;
- they are experiencing flashbacks or night-terrors;
- they become involved with drugs, alcohol, stealing, etc.;
- they pretend that nothing has happened.

How can adults help?

- Be familiar with the child's home background, including faith and culture, and share these religious and cultural beliefs with the child.
- Allow children to express their grief.
- Allow children time to fully understand and to come to terms with what has happened.
- Encourage children to ask questions and be consistent in the answers.
- Accept children's individual responses to what has happened (children are not a homogenous group).

- Keep routines as normal as possible and encourage usual activities with peers.
- Involve children in ceremonies and rituals where possible.
- Explain the range of emotional responses associated with bereavement.
- Encourage young children to engage in play.
- Help children's peer group to understand what has happened.
- Help children to organise their memories of the person.

Suicide

On the 28 December 1984, Jill died, aged 15 years, on the Liverpool to Manchester railway line. She told her parents that she was taking the dog for a walk, tied him in a safe place and threw herself under a train. She left a letter.

Dear Mummy,

Please don't waste too much effort on a large funeral after all the heartache I have caused you, it is hardly worth it. I am sorry that it has happened at Christmas. I killed myself because I had made a mess of so many things. I know you feel that isn't true, but it is. It was never your fault. I love you and Daddy very dearly, always remember that. I could just not get my act together, that's all. My future didn't seem very attractive. I think I was just one hell of a cracked up person. I've always felt inferior. I could never talk to anyone and know they had respected what I had said. Maybe I didn't let it show before because then I was younger and adulthood seemed a long way away and I thought as I got older my thoughts would change. Sadly they didn't.

Always remember me as you thought I was, not as a stupid person, which is how I feel about myself. I cannot not kill myself after writing this. (Sorry.)

Love, Jill
(your disobedient daughter)

Suicide is arguably the most complex of all human behaviours. The Bible records the suicides of Samson and Judas Iscariot and as early as 400CE Saint Augustine taught that suicidal behaviour was sinful because it violated the sixth commandment, 'Thou shalt not kill'. By the sixth century CE the Roman Catholic Church had established punishment for the relatives of a person who had committed suicide including forbidding burial of suicide victims in consecrated ground. Sometimes the bodies of relatives who had committed suicide were dragged behind carts. By the mid-eighteenth century Merian, a French physician, declared suicide to be the result of emotional illness and by the early part of the twentieth century Freud described suicidal behaviour as the result of a person's anger or aggression turned 'inwards'.

Today attitudes towards suicidal people range from impatience to pity, compassion or contempt for the weakness or mental instability of the suicidal person. Research suggests that adverse environmental factors may influence suicidal behaviour (Pfeffer 1986) with family breakdown playing a major factor in adolescent suicide. Children may commit suicide as an impulsive act not realising the irreversible nature of death (Wass and Stillion 1988).

Theoretical models of suicide

Although suicide has been the subject of study for many years, the reasons for a person taking their own life are not completely clear. Theories generally relate to two schools of thought, namely sociological and psychological.

Sociological models

Sociological models seek to find an explanation for suicide within social groupings. These models are largely based on the work of Durkheim.

Psychological models

Psychological models suggest various groups of people are at increased risk and suggest factors which might contribute to the individual act. Freud developed the earliest psychological explanations.

Suicide statistics are of doubtful accuracy because coroners are often reluctant to deliver a verdict of intentional death. However the most common factor in suicide is the intention to harm oneself and about a third of young people who commit suicide do so without warning and leave no clues as to why they ended their life. Other people like Jill in the opening paragraph tell people about their suicidal thoughts and then take their lives. Yet another group attempt suicide and survive with perhaps a greater risk of completing the act at a future date.

Some facts

- Suicide ranks as the third leading cause of death amongst adolescents.
- Males are four times more likely to commit suicide than females.
- Adolescents who have attempted suicide are significantly more likely than the general adolescent population to ultimately kill themselves.
- Suicidal thoughts or attempts are more likely to be known to peers than to adults.

Because suicide is viewed by much of society as unacceptable and there is a stigma attached to it, families often feel unworthy or unable to ask for help. For many families, when a member commits suicide there are major problems left behind for the survivors. Not least, partners and children may feel confused about the relationship that they had with the deceased person. Why didn't they give any warning of what they were doing? Or, if warning and threats were given, why was it disbelieved or ignored? Trauma experienced by children who survive the suicide of someone they know or someone close to them may be particularly severe because:

- the event was probably sudden and seldom anticipated;
- the death may have been violent;
- the nature of the death may accentuate feelings of remorse or guilt;
- survivors may experience a sense of loss of control in their lives;
- societal responses are often negative and judgemental.

Dyregrov (1991) believes that suicide creates a difficult situation for both bereaved adults and children. He says suicide challenges children's thoughts about what people can do and touches upon their own destructive impulses, their helplessness and their independence. For children, the reality that somebody can take their own life may make them feel deserted and let down. Even more distressing perhaps is the child who has discovered the body. Whatever the circumstances, those left after a suicide often experience complicated grief, especially if the death was caused through violent means such as hanging or shooting. Even young children may have fantasies about what happened, feel responsible for the event or, at worst, harbour thoughts that their own life is not worth living.

Raphael (1984) emphasises that in connection with adolescence, suicide often results in shame, stigma and guilt. This is particularly so if the suicide has happened at the time when family relationships have been fraught or full of ambivalence.

Adolescent suicide

Suicide is a major cause of death, second only to road traffic accidents, in young people aged between 16 and 24 years, with white males at greatest risk. A high proportion of victims have suffered major life changes in the preceding year. Young men have a tendency to resort to violent suicide such as hanging or shooting with young women tending to overdose or slash their wrists with less risk of completion (Ritter 1989). A family history of suicide puts young people at greatest risk of taking their own lives. Kastenbaum (1997) indicates that over three quarters of people who commit suicide provide some indication of their intent, and where young people talk about taking their lives this should never be dismissed.

Where an adolescent confides suicidal thoughts or behaviour to a peer they may not be taken seriously or they may not respond because:

- they may feel their friend is placing them in a compromising position;
- they may have been sworn to secrecy;
- they may not take the threat seriously;
- they may not know where to get assistance.

Risk factors for suicide are the subject of much debate (Blumenthal 1988). There is some empirical evidence (Valente *et al.* 1988, Raphael 1984), which suggests that teenagers who have experienced the suicide of someone close to them may be at greater risk of taking their own lives. Dyregrov (1991) outlines several factors which should alert adults to children who may be contemplating ending their own life:

- pre-occupation with scenes of death or expressing suicidal thoughts;
- giving away prized possessions;
- appearance of peace, relief, contentment, especially following a period of unrest;
- sudden and extreme changes in eating habits;
- withdrawal from friends and family or other major behavioural changes, such as aggression;
- changes in sleeping patterns;
- changes in school performance.

Throughout this book we have discovered adults are often reluctant to share open and honest information with children. This is especially so when death occurs through suicide and children are given inadequate, incorrect explanations or told half-truths. Perhaps the most commonly asked question after suicide is 'Why?' and children will either pose this themselves or be surrounded by other people who do. Young people cannot live their lives in a vacuum where they are protected from situations that are difficult to handle.

How can adults help?

Where a child has experienced the suicide of someone known to them adults can help by:

- acknowledging the shock of what has happened;
- reassuring children they were not to blame;
- reassuring children life is worth living;
- giving children as much time as they need to adjust to life without the person who is no longer there;
- allowing children to feel angry;
- allowing children to talk about suicide and how they feel.

What can teachers do?

Adolescent suicides have a devastating impact on schools, families and the communities in which they occur. Schools have most contact with adolescents during the day and they may notice behavioural changes. Teachers should:

- take suicidal threats seriously;
- be non-judgemental, providing an open listening environment;
- familiarise themselves with support groups within their community;
- provide young people with information about support services.

Summary

Adjusting to bereavement through death is often described as a series of orderly stages, yet children and adults experience a myriad of emotional responses that include a large number of interrelated thoughts, feelings and behaviours. Children's responses to death differ from those of adults in several ways, largely because their capacity to make sense of the event may be limited.

There is a considerable body of evidence to suggest that psychiatric disorders are more common in people who have been bereaved both as children and in adulthood.

Young people may feel disempowered in their emotional expression if adults 'disenfranchise' their grief or in circumstances where they suffer bereavement 'overload'. Bereavement is particularly traumatic when it is violent or unexpected. Sudden death such as suicide challenges children's perceptions about what people can do. It may also touch upon their own destructive impulses, their helplessness and their independence. If young people experience a threat to their own life, intense psychological reactions may emerge. Furthermore, preventable death may exacerbate the severity of a child's grief if they embark in searching for a determinant to which they may attach blame.

CHAPTER 6

The trauma of chronically ill and life-limited children

In 1995 Armstrong-Dailey estimated there were approximately seven million children world-wide who were seriously or chronically ill. Chronic diseases are a group of conditions that vary in the extent to which they represent a threat to a child's life and the quality of everyday activities. Thus a child with diabetes is likely to feel relatively well as long as she or he receives regular insulin, although there may be a risk of long-term complications in future life. Children with asthma are likely to experience some interludes of poor health although on a day to day basis they are able to lead normal lives. However the child with renal failure or cancer may live under what Massey (1985) calls a 'constant shadow'.

The likelihood of children experiencing trauma through chronic illness is dependent on several factors such as whether or not the illness is life threatening, the visibility of the condition, the impact on mobility and the quality of support received by the child in their family.

Children's understanding of illness

Children's understanding of illness differs at various stages of their cognitive development from early childhood to late adolescence, with a systematic progression in their understanding of illness related to age. Very young children typically perceive the causation of illness as magical or because they have transgressed rules. By the end of the primary phase illness may be attributed to germs. By early adolescence children understand that there are multiple causes of their sickness.

> When my baby brother was first diagnosed, I spent a lot of time helping to look after him. I decided because of that, I would be a physiotherapist when I grew up. That way I should be able to help other people too.

Among children at greatest risk to school absenteeism and poor academic performance are those with a chronic illness. They are vulnerable not only because of their medical condition, but because of the effects of the illness on their self concept and social interaction. For young people who take responsibility for their personal care, treatment can be extremely onerous. Changed body image is also a constant reminder to the child that he or she is ill and it may well affect the way that other people in school respond.

The work of Eiser and Havermans (1994) has contributed to an understanding of chronic illness on children's life goals and achievements. In a secondary school context chronic illness has been shown to include an increased risk of social isolation, poor attitude to academic study, truancy and school absence.

> If I can't have babies because of the disease, then how well I do at school is more important to me than it is for my friends. I want my life to have been worthwhile. (Maggie, aged 14)

Parents

Parenting takes an inordinate amount of time – and the demands escalate where a child has a chronic condition. During the period of illness, families have to come to terms with the knowledge that a previously healthy child has a chronic illness with no available cure. The period following the diagnosis of a very sick child is particularly critical and this is reflected in research findings (Vandvick and Eckblad, 1991).

Although in some conditions such as leukaemia a child may be considered medically cured if they survive five years or more after all treatment ends, parents may always experience a degree of unease about their child's health. Concerns appear to heighten when the child reaches significant milestones such as birthdays or the anniversary of the original diagnosis.

> I hear other parents worrying about their child's safety on school trips but for me it is more about the chance she should get ill again or that the drugs may inhibit her development. (Mother of a child in remission from cancer)

Socio-demographic factors

The socio-economic status of families is known to impact on the psychological and educational development of children. Parental reactions to illness often vary with their social and professional status, e.g. high achieving professional parents may have high expectations for their children that are shattered by the diagnosis of chronic or fatal illness or disability (Brown 1999). Birth order, sex of siblings, age spacing and family size have been a focus of studies concerning sibling development. In many families older siblings assume roles of caregivers and in Breslau's (1982) study, older siblings of chronically ill children were reported by their mothers and teachers to demonstrate higher rates of behavioural problems.

Family adaptive patterns

Mothers

The work of authors such as Hobfoll (1991) suggests that much of the burden of care for a chronically sick child falls heavily on mothers. Levels of maternal stress including anxiety and health problems remain high throughout periods of treatment (Kupst 1992). Mothers of pre-school children appear to experience greatest distress.

Fathers

According to Eiser (1993) fathers respond differently from mothers to the diagnosis of chronic disease in their child and they are less likely to suffer from psychological ill health than their partners. Eiser attributes this in part to less involvement in the everyday care of the child and reduced understanding about the disease.

Although fathers may not play a leading role in caring for their sick child, evidence suggests they play a crucial supporting role with their presence being vital in supporting the effects of chronic childhood disease on the mothers' mental health (Nagy and Ungerer 1990).

Life-limited and life-threatened children

Just as hopefulness and despair oscillate, so an appreciation of the time left oscillates with anger at how little of it there is. These polarities seem to exemplify the extremes of life and death itself; without one we could not have the other, and by attempting to embrace this polarity we are more able to relieve the fluctuating feelings and awarenesses of the dying child. (Judd 1989)

Spinetta (1984) concludes that a terminally ill child's level of trauma is markedly higher than that of a chronically or seriously ill child. Judd (1989) refers to childhood death as 'out of season'. In Great Britain, approximately 15,000 children and young people under the age of 20 die each year. Life-threatening illness plunges children into a confusing and previously unknown world, where people speak in medical jargon, and they are subjected to painful treatment and uncertainty. Normal routines are shattered and relationships turned upside down. In short, Doka's (1993) definition of a life-threatening illness as 'a condition which endangers life or has significant risk to death' falls short of describing what happens to a child and their family. Doka is however very helpful in describing the phases of life-threatening illness.

Phase 1: Pre-diagnosis – This period prior to diagnosis is often one when the seriousness of the condition is suspected.

Phase 2: Diagnostic – During this phase the illness is named and the reality of possible death is faced for the first time. It is a time of exceeding stress for families who often say that they experience a 'first death' at the time of diagnosis.

Phase 3: Chronic – This phase is generally marked by extensive medical treatment and often physical changes in the child. Families commonly deny the severity of the disease as they struggle to keep life as normal as possible. It is a time when parents need to begin to grieve the loss of normality in their lives.

Phase 4: Terminal – The illness has now progressed so that the inevitable outcome is death. Treatment is directed at pain relief, and aggressive intervention in order to maintain life is abandoned.

Anxiety about death is an issue for life-limited children although it is only during the last three decades that children's conceptual understanding and emotional response to their impending death has been studied. As recently as 1960 clinicians such as Knudson and

Natterson advocated that children should be protected from the reality. It was the pioneering work of practitioners such as Bluebond-Langner (1978) which prompted a revision of this perspective.

Children's understanding of life-threatening illness

Some researchers (Judd 1989) are of the opinion that although children may not have reached conceptual understanding of death, most are aware that something is physically wrong with their body. Adult theories which suggest that if children are unaware of the seriousness of their illness they will not be frightened are refuted by those who work with life-threatened children (Brown 1994, Waechter 1971). Children in hospitals or hospices where other young people are dying or have died, seem to show an enhanced awareness of death (and in some cases increased anxiety). Brown (1999) tells of children with AIDS and HIV on a paediatric ward of a hospital who were aware of memorial services and were angry that the adults who surrounded them were able to live normal lives outside the hospital. Among another group of youngsters on the oncology ward of the same hospital was a child who had heard the words such as 'kill' and 'invade' in relation to the therapy given to treat her disease. Understandably she had fantasies about warfare and was constantly checking she was not being attacked.

Bluebond-Langner (1995) says children who are life-limited or life-threatened have a more mature understanding of death than their healthy peers. This process involves encounters with illness that are paralleled by changes in their self-perception. First the child understands they are seriously ill and gradually moves towards a realisation of acute, chronic and fatal sickness (Table 6.1). It is important to recognise however that these phases are not clear-cut stages. They may overlap and in some cases be delayed by pathological grief. **Stage 1** is dependent on observing how other people respond and hearing what they say. After receiving treatment and visiting hospitals or clinics the child reaches **Stage 2** which often includes a remission in the illness. After the first relapse, **Stage 3** is reached and as a result of several more relapses and remissions the child realises at **Stage 4** this is the pattern in their life. When the child realises that someone else has died they parallel their own experience and **Stage 5** is achieved.

Table 6.1

Diagnosis	1	2	3	4	5
	My illness is serious	I am taking powerful drugs and they have side effects	I know why I am having the treatment	I am suffering relapses and remissions	The pattern of relapses and remissions will end in death

(Based on Herbert 1996)

As children's illness progresses they often refer less to treatment and more to how the time which they have left will be spent. Certainly some children have an urgent need to achieve ambition. They plead to be taken outside hospitals and hospices for social events even though they are too ill to fully participate in their chosen activity. Ambitions seem to monopolise many of the conversations between children and adults. Often they demonstrate challenging behaviour reflecting what Bluebond-Langner (1995) calls disengaging people in a rehearsal for the final separation of death.

While in the experience of the authors most children who are dying have shown an awareness of what is happening to them before the event happens, the acquisition and assimilation of knowledge may be a prolonged process. Where children are told they are dying before death is imminent, Bluebond-Langner (1995) refers to the process as one of 'internalisation'. Where they are not told directly but learn what is happening, the same author refers to this as a process of 'discovery'.

How children are likely to respond to the news of their own life limitation will determine the way in which they are told the news. Adults should:

- help children to express their fears and concerns;
- help children to communicate what they know about their illness;
- help children to express their own preferences and needs.

As children progress through the stages of their illness, their view of themselves changes as they accumulate more information. It is a process which is dependent on experience rather than age.

Sandy, aged six, drew a picture of herself as she would be in her coffin after she died. When she gave it to the Play Coordinator in the hospice she started to weep uncontrollably saying she was frightened about how she would get out of the box when she woke up.

Life-limited adolescents

Adolescence is a journey of discovery, turmoil, challenge, experimentation, ambivalence, egocentricity, confidence and self-doubt combined with unfolding changes physically, emotionally and intellectually. Coping with a life-threatening illness is a monumental undertaking. Unlike young children, adolescents generally perceive death as irreversible. Therefore acceptance of personal death is particularly difficult because for many young people their lives are orientated towards the future. This can, in some cases, lead to unrealistic thoughts about the time ahead.

Keith was 18 when he was admitted to his local hospice for respite care during the terminal phase of his illness. Although he had spent many hours researching the likely prognosis of his disease on the Internet he told his key worker he planned to take part in a sponsored walk of the Great Wall of China the following year.

This young adult was expressing his hopes and dreams to his key worker, although he knew he was unlikely to live more than a few weeks. Conversely Sally, debilitated by the end stage of cystic fibrosis, became distressed when her parents expressed no recognition of the fact that she was dying. She told her nurses that she knew she was dying. Staff validated her feelings by reassuring her she would not be left alone and asking her whether she would like to tell her parents she knew her life was coming to an end. Sally agreed and asked that her family came to the hospice the following day so that she could say goodbye to them. Through gathering her family together before she died, Sally was dealing with unfinished business and feeling a sense of control.

Meeting the individual needs of children

In working with life-threatened children, professionals are frequently faced with the following questions: What does the child want to know? What does the child need to know? What can the child understand? Taking into account the child's developmental understanding, these questions might be translated as follows (Brown 1999):

Babyhood and toddlers' needs

- helping cope with pain;
- frequent physical contact (or touching) from primary carers;
- frequent contact with the voices of primary carers;
- normal routines as far as possible;
- opportunities to play and to interact with family members.

Pre-school children

- reassurance that any separation from primary carers is unavoidable;
- reassurance that the illness is not a form of punishment;
- open communication in easily understood language;
- explanations about medical procedures;
- constant reassurance about love and care from their family;
- access to communication which will help indicate levels of pain or distress;
- routines which are normal as possible;
- opportunities to interact with peers and families where possible;
- opportunities to communicate fears and concerns.

Children aged 5–7 years

- open and honest communication about the nature of the illness;
- opportunities to communicate preferences, needs, fears and concerns;
- maintenance of familiar routines as far as possible;
- constant reassurance of the love and care of family members, peers and friends;
- access to communication which will help them articulate levels of pain or anxiety;
- access to educational activities and hobbies;
- liaison with school.

Children aged 7–9 years

- open and honest communication about the nature and inevitable outcome of their illness;

- opportunities to express their own opinions, wishes and anxieties;
- constant reassurance of the love and care of key people in their lives;
- freedom to make decisions about their own pain control and care;
- opportunities to express their awareness of how family members are responding;
- maintenance of familiar cultural or religious traditions.

Adolescents

- opportunities to express fears and concerns for self and to family members;
- privacy, especially when undergoing personal care;
- opportunities to maintain autonomy and independence for as long as possible;
- support from peer groups as well as family members;
- involvement in decisions regarding their care;
- maintenance of familiar cultural and religious traditions.

Families of life-limited children

The strategies which families adopt for dealing with any crisis will generally be an indicator of how they will cope with a life-threatening illness. Families need not only to witness that their child is cared for, but also to experience how their own emotional, psychological and spiritual needs are met.

There are several phases which most parents who are caring for a dying child will experience:

- numbness on hearing the news of the child's prognosis: this may be accompanied by feelings of shock, disbelief and denial;
- yearning for the normality of life before the news was heard which may be accompanied by acute feelings of searching, crying, reminiscing, anger and guilt;
- hopelessness and despair which may be accompanied by feelings of loneliness, helplessness, depression and anxiety.

Supporting the whole family

Family communication patterns appear to be critical in determining how well families cope with illness, since the most valuable sources of support are embedded in their relationships, open-parenting styles, and philosophy. Evidence from a number of studies suggests the families' cultural, social and educational background also influences how they cope. Furthermore the findings of Phillimore *et al.* (1994) show that economic status in families may be a factor in coping with bereavement.

Culling (1988) suggests that families who are able to communicate their feelings collectively facilitate adaptation to life-threatening and terminal illness. Children look to their family for support especially when situations are unknown and unexpected. Typically they mirror the coping strategy shown by their parents (Moody and Moody 1991). Stephenson (1985) contrasts closed and open family communication systems which operate in the face of death. Rigidity and tightly defined roles together with strict thought and behaviour patterns characterise closed family systems. Generally the significance and impact of death is not openly acknowledged or discussed and family members may be isolated. Conversely the open family system functions in what Stephenson calls a 'nurturing' environment where the impact of death is openly recognised and adults express their thoughts and feelings, encouraging children to do likewise. He describes this as 'parents and children facilitating each other's grieving'.

Within each of the phases of illness experienced by the child, the family will also have to develop strategies for adjusting and coping. These will differ from the diagnostic phase to the terminal phase but they may include:

- adjusting to medical intervention and institutional treatments;
- developing strategies to manage stress;
- communicating effectively with professional people and carers;
- preparing for death and saying 'goodbye';
- maintaining the family identity;
- preserving relationships with partners and friends;
- expressing emotions and fears;
- accepting the finality of death.

How can professionals support children?

Professionals can:

- encourage open and honest communication between adults and the child and their family;
- advocate on behalf of the young person with respect to ethical dilemmas;
- communicate any preferences or wishes expressed by the child to families and primary carers;
- encourage children to complete unfinished business and say 'goodbye';
- respond to the young person's requests for any support.

Supporting the siblings of dying children

Children's needs are sometimes overlooked by adults who are locked in their own grief. Because of the importance of emotional bonding and attachments, the death of a sibling may have a profound effect on surviving children. How they respond will largely depend on what they understand about death and what they have been taught and experienced in their families. Almost all children will need help during the first two years after a death to:

- understand their parents' grief;
- communicate what they are feeling;
- express their sadness and longing, especially at times such as celebrations, birthdays and holidays.

There is a considerable body of evidence which suggests that psychiatric disorder is significantly more common in people who have been bereaved both in childhood and in adult life (Black 1989). In Lansdown and Goldman's (1988) study of 28 children whose brothers and sisters had died, the majority were found to have behavioural and emotional difficulties and low self-esteem.

Most siblings will welcome involvement in their brother or sister's care. However, like their parents, they may be reluctant or have little opportunity to communicate their confusion and anxiety. Hospitals, hospices and support services are responding by providing group meetings to provide opportunities for peers to meet together.

What do siblings need?

- The family kept together where possible.
- Information about what is happening.
- Reassurance that they were not to blame.
- Explanations using language which is accessible and clearly understood.
- Opportunities to express emotions and reassurance that their feelings are normal.
- Adults who will be brave enough to share their grief.
- Reassurance of their value and how much they are loved.

How can adults help?

- Keep the family together as far as possible.
- Reassure surviving siblings they were not to blame.
- Explain what happened, using language which is accessible and clearly understood.
- Give siblings opportunities to express their emotions and reassurance that anything that they might feel is normal.
- Share grief with children.
- Reassure siblings how much they are loved.

Summary

Chronic diseases are a group of conditions that vary in the extent to which they represent a threat to a child's life and the quality of his or her everyday activities. The likelihood of children experiencing trauma through their illness is dependent on factors such as the effect of the illness on mobility and the quality of support received by the child and their family.

Children's understanding of illness differs according to their stage of cognitive development with a systematic progression in their understanding of illness, related to age.

During the period of illness families have to come to terms with the knowledge that a previously healthy child is sick with no available cure. Parental reactions vary according to their professional and economic status and research suggests that the burden of care falls heavily on mothers. Levels of maternal stress are high. Although fathers may not play a leading role in caring for their sick child, evidence suggests they play a crucial supporting role within the family, with particular reference to sustaining the mental health of their partner.

Each year in Great Britain approximately 15,000 children and young people under the age of 20 die of a life-threatening illness. Research suggests that a terminally ill child's level of trauma is markedly higher than that of a chronically or seriously ill child.

Young people's conceptual and emotional response to their impending death reveals they are best supported when their own needs and the wishes of their families are taken into account.

Within each stage of the child's illness, the family will have to develop strategies for adjusting and coping. Adults who are locked in their own grief may overlook the needs of brothers and sisters. The extent to which siblings experience trauma depends largely on what they understand about death and the communication systems present in their families.

CHAPTER 7

Faith and cultural aspects of care

Religious and cultural lifestyles are central to many families in Great Britain. They tend to become even more important at key points in people's lives, shared family occasions, or in the face of adversity. Few schools or caring communities would intentionally cause offence to ethnic minority families, but where carers know very little about other people's sensitivities and values, the quality of experience offered may at best be impoverished and at worst lead to individuals feeling marginalised and insignificant.

Any traumatic event is likely to involve members of religious and ethnic communities. People from black and ethnic minority backgrounds account for approximately five per cent of the United Kingdom population. As yet there is very little data concerning the incidence of minority ethnic children experiencing Post-Traumatic Stress Disorder. This chapter considers aspects of race, ethnicity, culture, religion and spirituality that should be addressed by schools and caring services. It also sets out to provide a base of information from which to discuss the needs and wishes of children and families, with particular reference to trauma that results in death. Each trauma is unique and will require creative, immediate and flexible responses. When people are members of faith communities there may be some specific requirements and these are set out in the section 'Rites and rituals surrounding death'.

Spirituality

'Spirituality is a dimension within every person – religious, atheist, or humanist' (Stoll 1989). There will be differences in the approaches taken to the idea of 'spiritual' by different individuals, for example by those with religious belief and non-believers. For those with a strong religious faith, the spiritual is very much at the heart of life; for many religious people, there is no concept of the secular as distinct from the spiritual; for some who may make no religious profession, it may be hard to accept the very term 'spiritual'.

An Indian proverb describes a person as 'a house with four rooms, a physical, a mental, an emotional and a spiritual place', advising that each room should be entered each day 'even if only to keep it aired' (Godden 1989). Compton (1998) describes the traumatised child as dis-spirited although Cattermole (1990) believes that children's spiritual growth can exist within the context of suffering and distress. The authors have often spoken of traumatised children as 'down-spirited'.

Spiritual aspects of care

Part of what makes us human is a need to make sense of life by plotting our mark on a spiritual and cultural map. Indeed our hopes and dreams may be shaped by where we perceive ourselves to be on such a map. Spiritual and religious care involves attending to families' beliefs, including their fears, anxieties and hopes. The way in which society responds to individual people reflects not only its qualities of compassion and caring but also its sense of justice and its commitment to enhancing the quality of human experience.

Until children have their fears and hopes affirmed, the totality of their person is not addressed and cared for. To be cut off from hope is to feel abandoned. Although a child's trust in the predictability and certainty of life may have been shattered, they seek for purpose and value in the midst of uncertainty.

More than thirty years ago Piaget's model of child development described the way in which children make sense of their world and how their individual development progressed through logical stages. At the heart of good holistic care lies an acknowledgement of children's individuality and the uniqueness of their development.

For children from minority ethnic families, care which is matched to their individual needs is tremendously important because being 'different' has often been associated with deficit. Often children grapple with their anxiety alone because they are fearful the trauma they are feeling will be brushed aside.

Holistic care

> Spiritual and cultural are interwoven; they are dependent on the other, rather like an adult and a child. (Bacon 1994)

In the nursing profession, holistic care that embraces a balance between mind, body and spirit for the health of a person, has been advocated for many years. Narayanasamy (1993) says 'mind, body and spirit are inseparable and function as an integrated unit within the whole person in each dimension … affecting and being affected by others'.

In order to support a planned and coherent approach to provide for children's holistic development, all members of caring communities need to have a shared understanding of the values that the organisation is promoting. The process by which this understanding develops will be informed by statutory requirements and documentary guidance. However the concerns and interests of children and their families also need to be taken into account.

Racial discrimination against the minority, by the majority, is about power and oppression – it is a dehumanising experience. The Children Act 1989 makes it unlawful to ignore a child's racial origin and cultural, ethnic and linguistic background in the process of any decision making.

Families have needs that are specific to them. Some will have never experienced long-term distress or uncertainty before. Most will have some hopes and expectations of the people who care for them. Although these expectations vary for each family, they may include:

- hoping for the availability of carers and accessibility to them;
- hoping for support matched to each individual family member;

- hoping that professionals will support and empower them in the face of adversity, rather than diminishing their confidence;
- hoping that care will be reliable, consistent and honest;
- hoping that professionals will give them sufficient time to absorb what has happened to them;
- hoping that professionals will support their needs to do things their way;
- hoping that professionals will help them to fulfil their own expectations of recovery from the trauma.

Ethnicity and culture

The Commission for Racial Equality uses the term 'ethnic minorities' believing that cultural and religious differences are important. Thus there is a tendency to use the notion of 'ethnicity' rather than race, implying shared or common features such as language, religion and origin. McGoldrick (1982) describes an ethnic group as containing persons who perceive themselves as alike. However the word ethnic is often abused by referring to non-white populations as ethnic groups as if other communities do not have an ethnicity.

Ethnicity includes culture. Culture was defined as early as 1871 when Tylor described it as 'that complex whole which includes knowledge, belief, art, morals, laws, customs and any other capabilities acquired by man as a member of society'. Anthropologists describe culture as the plans and rules that people use to interpret their world and to interact within it.

Although many people have similar cultural backgrounds, there will be important and distinct differences in culture between people from different communities. There are also many religious groups that will have their own philosophical and social systems.

Religion

Religion is a system of beliefs, rituals and behaviour and religions, groups of people with shared beliefs and behaviour that are directed towards a common goal. There is great diversity of religious belief and cultural practice among different communities. Some people are extremely devout and find a focus of their lives in religion; others have discarded most external signs of religious practice but still have a strong faith; some have no faith but keep the values of religious traditions in which they were brought up. Often the complexities and richness of a religion are more apparent from the stance of the believer. For many people, religious observance is expressed through everyday practices such as ablution, style of dress or dietary adherence. Religious rituals offer a person a chance to participate in religious behaviour without declaring the extent of their beliefs.

Religion may offer meaning in the face of the incomprehensible. But it is not unusual for people to be angry about what life has dealt them, and angry with God 'if God exists'. Sometimes it is as if people imagine themselves as having crossed a forbidden line so that they have drawn punishment upon themselves.

There are many examples that illustrate how faith can offer children solace and hope in the future (see Figures 7.1 and 7.3).

When I die my soul will go to Allah. My body will stay in the ground.

Sabina's family are Muslim. She knows she has a life-threatening illness but she is reassured that after death she will enter the gates of heaven.

Figure 7.1

Kennedy (1995) writes,

There is great potential for child survivors to benefit from 'speaking' to God about their pain, anger and hurt via special liturgies and worship. Such worship must allow the child to 'be real'. All emotions, beliefs and feelings should be accepted and incorporated into the liturgy and worship. If a child wishes to say that they hate God, then so be it. This allows them space to vent their hurt and pain against God, whom they often perceive has let them down, and betrayed them just as their perpetrator has.

Death and dying in world religions

Death arouses great curiosity. Questions about the meaning and purpose of life are accompanied by questions of what happens next. Religions seek to give answers to these mysteries of human existence. For some people death may cause them to question long-held feelings, beliefs and meanings. Sometimes people seek to determine an explanation of their personal tragedy through their religion. This may involve questions about sins they have committed, laws they have broken or faith they have lost.

All major religions teach there is some kind of continuity or survival after death. They also reassure mourners by helping to make sense of death and provide shape and meaning to the process of grieving. Children reflect their cultural and ethnic backgrounds in their understanding of death but their age is not necessarily an accurate predictor of how much they know or believe (see Figure 7.2).

No tradition should be reduced to a few sentences and essentially it is impossible for non-believers to fully understand another person's faith. Professionals must be prepared to live with the discomfort of feeling deskilled and inadequate and to learn to let families show them the way. There is value however in having an insight into some of the beliefs and rituals which guide the steps of people faced with crisis and loss.

'When I die God will look after me' – Charlotte, aged 6

Charlotte has not yet reached an understanding of the permanence of her death. She talks about getting in and out of her 'box' but is reassured. God will give her physical hugs and food.

Figure 7.2

The Buddhist community

There are three main schools of Buddhism, each strand demonstrating diversity of practice. Followers strive to walk in the path of the Buddha, following his example. Through Buddhism people attempt to achieve liberation from the cycle of rebirth in which all living things are caught. Buddhism teaches that nothing is permanent and that suffering and unhappiness are to be expected in earthly life. Buddhists would however hope to face adversity with an attitude of quiet and calm acceptance. Therefore anything that encourages them towards this is likely to be appreciated.

The Chinese community

Chinese religions embrace Buddhism, Confucianism and Taoism. Therefore it is difficult to be definitive about Chinese belief and practice. However, many of the practices associated with death and mourning rites are not dissimilar for those within mainstream Buddhism.

The Christian community

Three main movements are embraced by the Christian tradition, namely the Orthodox Church, the Catholic Church and the Protestant Church. There is enormous diversity of practice within these churches but at the heart of Christianity is the figure of Jesus as the model for human living. Faced with adversity Christians often find compelling support in the hope of salvation and of life to come. Bacon (1994) describes the Christian gospel as 'connecting with helplessness, abandonment and grieving'. In many Christian communities ordained persons minister to faith members and at times of tragedy and grief they would strive to support families in the context of the fellowship of the church, providing comfort and solace.

The Hindu community

Hinduism demonstrates diversity in devotion, sacred writing and practice. The faith is permeated by deities that are manifestations of one reality, Brahman, the Supreme Being whose existence is innate in all living things. Life is a continuing flux of birth and rebirth bound by belief that conduct in this life determines the condition of the next life. Liberation from the cycle of birth and rebirth can only be achieved through endeavour. Belief in rebirth is based upon the conviction that the soul is immortal and indestructible. In the days following a death the whole family will mourn for a period of between 11 and 13 days and they will rely on the support from their religious community.

The Jewish community

Judaism in the United Kingdom is divided into three main traditions, namely Hasidic, Orthodox and Progressive (combining Reform and Liberal). There are also many non-affiliated Jews who may adhere to some festivals and take part in community events but they are not generally religious. Judaism has a long concept of monotheism teaching a wide range of beliefs about after life. Some Jews believe in bodily resurrection and others in an internal soul. Most believe in some kind of after life but the main focus of belief concerns a Messianic Age when the souls of the departed will be reunited with their bodies. Jewish communities provide comfort and practical support to bereaved families.

The Muslim community

Islam was revealed to the prophet Mohammed. There are many cultural variations within Islam. However in general terms, Islam is a way of life and a person who submits to Allah the Creator, can achieve peace of body and of mind. Islam teaches that Allah created life and that humankind is the highest form of creation. Although people have free will, when they die, their earthly deeds are accountable before Allah on the Day of Judgement. On this day a person is either rewarded and enters a stage of blessing or heaven or they are punished by a stage of punishment or hell. Faced with adversity many Muslims express solidarity within their community and friends and relations play an important part in supporting families.

The Sikh community

In Sikhism references to death are often found associated with birth and the words Janum (birth) and Moran (death) generally occur together. According to Sikh belief humankind is not born sinful but in the grace of God which gives the soul the opportunity to become 'God in Flesh'. A person is not born free. They are born to be free through breaking the cycle of life in order for their soul to rise to communion with Eternal God. Thus, life is mortal, but the spirit is immortal. Sikhism teaches that the Day of Judgement will come to everyone immediately after death. It also teaches that heaven and hell are not locations but are symbolically represented by joy or sorrow, bliss and agony, light and darkness. Hell is seen as a corrective experience in which people suffer in continuous cycles of birth and death. The burden may only be thrown off by living a perfect life. In Sikhism there are two distinct doctrines about rebirth. Firstly, when the soul passes from one life to another in spiritual progress, Nirvana (or perfection). This is eventually achieved through reincarnation. Secondly, rebirth in animal life is punishment. In striving for Nirvana it is believed that the soul of the Sikh passes through a number of stages and moral conditions. For about ten days after a funeral relatives will gather, either at home or the gurdwara, for the completion of the reading of the holy book, the Guru Granth Sahib.

Rites and rituals surrounding death

For people with a strong religious conviction the meaning of life and the meaning of death are inextricably bound. In many faiths, life is a preparation for death and the life to come. It is extremely difficult to summarise the most common rituals and ceremonies which occur at the time of death or immediately afterwards. The information which follows attempts to raise awareness of some of the sensitivities that should be shown towards families of different faiths.

Buddhism

- Where possible, families will wish to be with the person who is dying. A religious teacher may be invited to talk to the person.

- The body will remain untouched until a priest arrives.
- Family members will stay together for as long as possible.
- The body will be washed after death and laid out, sometimes by members of the family or religious community.
- An environment will be appreciated which is as quiet as possible and conducive to prayer/meditation.
- A photograph of the deceased may be placed near the coffin.
- A period of between three and seven days will usually elapse before the funeral.
- Burial or cremation will depend on the school of Buddhism/country of origin.
- Periods of mourning vary according to the country of origin.

Chinese religions of Confucianism and Taoism

- Most families will wish that death occurs in the presence of the dying person's family.
- At the time of death families will wish the person to be facing a certain direction according to Fung Shui.
- After death the body will be washed and dressed before being placed in the coffin.
- Families will wear white or light coloured clothing as a symbol of mourning.
- Funerals usually take place a few days after death.
- The body may be buried or cremated.
- Single layer graves are preferable – cremated remains may be buried in cemeteries.
- Relatives (mourners) will usually prefer hot food.
- Mourning will continue for up to a year after death, with a special commemorative occasion at each anniversary of the death.

Christianity

- The dying person may wish to receive Holy Communion and/or the Sacrament of the Sick (or Sacrament of Reconciliation).
- The family may wish to say prayers thanking God for the life of the person and the life to come.
- Prayers may be said on behalf of the family and on behalf of the dying person.
- A quiet place will be appreciated in order for the family to pray or to talk with a minister or priest.
- The family will want to carry out the wishes of the dead person and to be able to make their own decisions with regard to burial or cremation. In some traditions Mass or Communion may be included in the funeral service.
- Although they are all Trinitarian Churches, Roman Catholics, Anglicans and Non-Conformists (Methodists, Baptists, Congregationalists, Presbyterians) have variations in their beliefs and practices.

Hinduism

- The dying person will wish to have someone with them. They may wish to lie on the floor and to sip Holy Ganges' water.

- The body will be washed after death by members of the religious community.
- The body will be wrapped in a white shroud or white clothes, except in the case of a young woman, who may be wrapped in a red sari.
- A gold coin or leaf from the sacred tulsi plant may be put in the mouth of the deceased person.
- Family members will wish to keep the body close to them or as close to the Hindu community as possible.
- There should be an opportunity for the family to talk to other family members or somebody from the religious community (they may prefer somebody of the same sex as themselves).
- The next of kin will wish to make the funeral arrangements. The first part of the ceremony may take place at home.
- The body will be cremated with the exception of children under three years old who will be buried.
- The eldest male in the family will play a key role in the funeral service.
- In India a period of 10 to 16 days is spent mourning. In Great Britain there may be rituals during the first year after death.

Islam

- If possible, the declaration of faith (Shahada) will be recited before death.
- A dying person will wish to have somebody with them.
- Family members will try to be together where possible.
- Post mortems will not take place except where demanded by civil law.
- The dead body will be washed three times and dressed in clean clothes. Family members will wish to wash themselves afterwards.
- The head of the deceased is turned onto the right shoulder and then positioned facing Makkah (south-east in the UK).
- The body is covered with a plain clean cloth.
- The next of kin will make the funeral arrangements. Islamic law requires friends and relations to feed mourners for three days after the death.
- Burial will take place as soon as possible and cremation will be forbidden.
- The body may be returned to the place of birth.
- In some cases the body may be embalmed.
- Apart from blood relatives the mourners will avoid bodily contact with persons of the opposite sex.
- Relatives may wish to visit the grave regularly on Fridays for up to 40 days after the death. Mourning ends with a meal and Qur'anic reading.
- Families will appreciate being provided with accommodation in a non-smoking and alcohol-free place.

Judaism

- It is usual for someone to be with the person at the time of death. Some Jews would wish for a rabbi to be present.

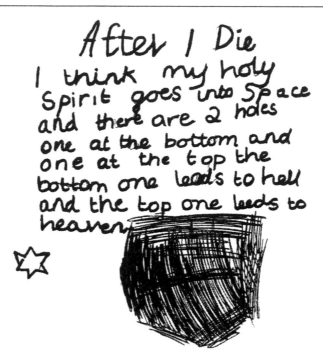

At age seven and a half, Harry has an understanding of what his faith community teaches about an after life

Figure 7.3

- Shema is said either by the person who is dying or by the relatives (the declaration of faith).
- The body is washed by members of the Jewish community (Orthodox).
- In the Orthodox tradition physical contact with the body will be avoided by members of the opposite sex.
- The body will be accompanied from the time of death to time of burial.
- The body will be buried as soon as possible after death, preferably within 25 hours (but not on the Sabbath or holy days).
- In Orthodox communities close family members will mourn for a period of 30 days after the death.
- In Orthodox communities close family members will refrain from attending celebrations for the period of mourning.
- At the end of the period of mourning a tombstone will be consecrated with a ceremony at the cemetery.

Sikhism

- Sikhs will wish to have somebody with them at the time of their death. They may wish to have portions of the Guru Granth Sahib read to them.

- After death the body will be washed before cremation and dressed by members of the family or members of the religious community.
- Sikhs will wish to wear the five Ks wherever possible, including a white turban for a man. Young women will be dressed in a red sari or a red shroud.
- The body will be covered with a clean white sheet and money or other gifts may be placed in the coffin.
- Sikhs will wish other people from outside their community to refrain from comforting them or having physical contact with them, for example hugging.
- Families may like to listen to readings from the Guru Granth Sahib for about ten days after the funeral.
- Families will appreciate accommodation in a non-smoking and alcohol-free environment.
- If the father of the family has died the eldest son may be given a turban to signify he is now head of the family.

The above are not exhaustive lists, and do not make allowances for groups within each religion who may have their own strong beliefs and rituals. Whatever their faith, people should not be coerced into an activity or ritual simply because it is considered to be the norm.

Summary

Any traumatic event is likely to involve members of religious and ethnic communities. For members of religious communities, faith may offer meaning in the face of circumstances which are incomprehensible. Death, or the threat of death, arouses curiosity and questions about the meaning and purpose of life. Many children and adults will turn to their faith to seek answers to these mysteries of human existence.

Each trauma is unique. Some families from faith and cultural backgrounds will have specific needs. Carers should develop their knowledge and understanding of faith and cultural contexts of care. Only then are they able to demonstrate an awareness of people's beliefs, fears, anxieties and hopes.

CHAPTER 8

Recovery from PTSD

Perhaps the most common question asked by PTSD survivors is 'When will I get better?' It is a perfectly natural question. If a person suffers an appendicitis or a broken leg there is a typical recovery period and there are definite stages before good health is regained. Stitches are removed or the plaster cast is taken off. With PTSD there are no such readily identifiable stages of recovery, and each individual's progress will be different.

Models of recovery

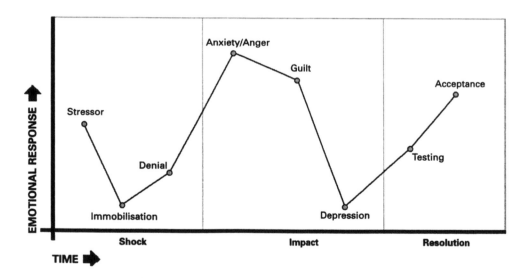

Figure 8.1 Model of PTSD recovery (after Williams 1993)

In Williams' (1993) model (Figure 8.1) the first phase of PTSD is described as the initial trauma (stressor) and the initial immobilisation and denial which are the main characteristics of this phase. This phase is the initial shock of the trauma.

The second phase, or impact phase, is characterised by chronic stress reactions. Flashbacks and all the associated symptoms are usually experienced during this phase.

The third stage is the recovery or adjustment phase. This involves the survivor 'testing' situations which were previously avoided because of their association with the original stressor. Finally, there is an acceptance of the trauma and an integration of the traumatic memory as part of a life-memory.

Unfortunately, in the experience of the authors, Williams' model falls far short of characterising the general stages of recovery by the PTSD survivor. The time scale is seldom clear – yet Williams' model suggests a regular recovery time. Williams' placing of symptoms such as anger and depression within the impact phase also gives an erroneous impression that anger is far more significant than depression. It suggests a set pattern of recovery, but fails to provide an accurate time scale for these phases. The model would appear to ask as many questions as it answers.

Horowitz (1979) also produced a model showing the phases of response following a trauma (Figure 8.2). The model extends from the initial outcry of the traumatic incident, through a state of denial, intrusive memories and working through what happened, until completion is reached. Horowitz advocates that there is a period of oscillation between states but that progress is made towards the person returning to the state before the occurrence of the event.

Once again, in our view, this model is far too simple, and does not tell the full story. Furthermore, it also assumes that eventually the impact of the trauma will disappear. More recent work suggests this is not the case (Kinchin 1998). Like a physical wound, which leaves some scar tissue as a reminder of the injury, victims of trauma incorporate the event into their life experience with psychological scarring.

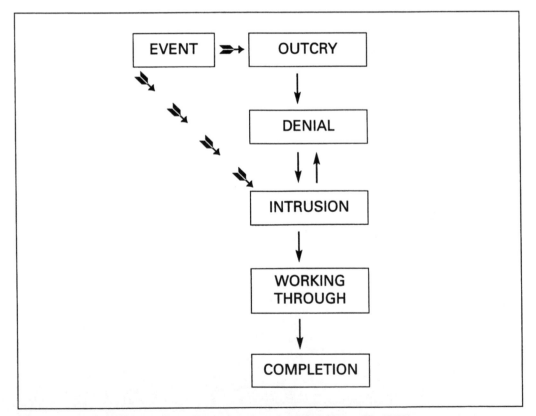

Figure 8.2 Phases of response following trauma (after Horowitz 1979)

In many ways, PTSD sufferers find themselves playing a game of emotional snakes and ladders. The game board represents the road to recovery, divided into one hundred squares. A series of ladders helps the person on the way towards recovery but between these ladders are the snakes which may take the victim backwards towards the start of the game, experiencing previous anguish and turmoil.

The snakes and ladders model of recovery

See Figure 8.3. The traumatic event takes place on square one. From this position recovery begins. Some survivors may shake the dice scoring five, four, three, and then one to reach square 100, thus achieving recovery in just four shakes of the dice. In less than four weeks these persons have recovered from the trauma and they do *not* go on to develop PTSD. Other survivors have to journey around the board going up the ladders and down the snakes as they slowly progress to the end of the game. Tragically, some people may never finish the game. Furthermore, some may never roll the correct number on the dice to finish exactly on square 100, or more tragically, they may give up and walk away from the game board taking unrelinquished trauma with them.

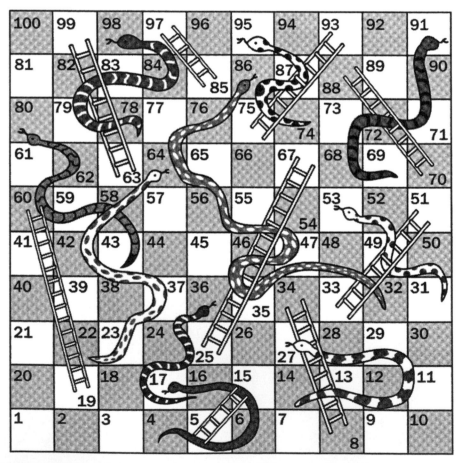

Figure 8.3 Snakes and ladders model of recovery (Kinchin 1994, 1998)

The game of snakes and ladders is very complex. Study the game board in detail. It is possible for a player to be on square 97, only to shake a one, two, five, five, five and one. These throws take a player back to square 4! Thankfully, on a true snakes and ladders board no snake can take a person all the way back to square one. So a person can finish the game in four moves, or can be taken back 94 squares in just six moves. Describing PTSD in such a way may aid a greater insight into the complicated road to recovery from PTSD. This analogy is probably more realistic than the very simple idea that recovery is a case of two steps forward and then one step back. Recovery is not smooth. Neither is it predictable and it will incorporate a wealth of stages which extend far beyond the models described by Williams and Horowitz.

Examples of snakes and ladders

Examples of snakes and ladders which might affect a person's recovery are described below.

Ladders

- Good medication, such as antidepressants, can be seen as an essential aid to recovery for many child survivors. The withdrawal of medication has to be slow and sympathetic or this 'ladder' can quickly become a 'snake'.
- Therapy which includes counselling, and any other form of support in which the child has confidence (Kinchin 1997).
- Relaxation techniques can be taught, and practised.
- Realisation that there is a 'trauma bond' or a feeling of empathy which exists between those who have suffered traumatic events. It is a realisation that 'you are not alone', and 'you are not going mad'.
- Individual or group support is an essential part of recovery.

Snakes

- Panic attacks can become a major 'snake' in the path of recovery. Because the fear of panic is so great many child survivors develop avoidance strategies in an attempt to stay away from anything which might cause a panic attack.
- Depression can manifest itself any time. A deep trough of depression can cause a survivor to walk away from the game board altogether. Consequently, this is the most dangerous 'snake' of all.
- Alcohol and non-prescribed drugs can act as an initial 'crutch', but dependency on these products can seriously hinder any real progress towards recovery. This is particularly true of adolescent survivors.
- Adverse publicity can heighten the state of a survivor's feelings of guilt.
- Anniversaries are often obstacles, but a successfully handled anniversary can also be turned into a very positive milestone towards recovery.
- Non-acceptance of PTSD by professionals and lay persons can be a serious problem for survivors who feel the severity of the traumatic response is being disregarded or belittled.

The examples above illustrate some of the events and issues which may affect children on the road to recovery. Many PTSD sufferers and their carers tend to set themselves goals or targets. Often these targets will be linked to the calendar:

'I will return to school by 1st June.'

'I want to have stopped sleeping with the *main light* on by Christmas.'

'I intend to go out shopping on my own during my school half-term holiday.'

Formulating goals and targets is a very good strategy provided the targets are within reach. If the target is too difficult, then the sufferer is in danger of setting unrealistic goals which serve no useful purpose. Rather, sufferers should be encouraged to set themselves sensible, attainable, targets. Dates for accomplishing tasks should be within a reasonable time scale. If the target is reached before the date, a treat may act as a positive reward. For children in particular, it is vital they are enabled to achieve small steps towards recovery.

Inevitably, some targets will not be achieved. Life is full of unpredictable events which may hinder progress. That's life! Therefore, unexpected events should be allowed for in the preparation of targets and breathing spaces need to be allowed between achieving a goal and embarking on the next hurdle. Targets are wonderful when they are achieved, but terrible if the child is defeated by them.

The snakes and ladders board can act as a helpful reminder to the child of their journey towards recovery. If he fails to reach a target, that failure does not drag him all the way back to square one. Even in failing, he has learned something about how best to set the next target.

Full recovery

It is not necessary to reach square 100 on the snakes and ladders board to have recovered from PTSD. Indeed, we suggest that in some cases reaching square 100 is not possible. Witnessing or being involved in a seriously traumatic event affects the rest of a survivor's life. This may require a person rethinking life-goals or life-values. Perhaps it would be useful to consider full recovery as anything beyond square 91 on the game board. Thus, if we return to the example of a broken leg cited earlier, there is always the thought in the back of a person's mind that the leg could break again. Likewise with PTSD, some of the symptoms could be awakened if triggers occur. Therefore, reaching the top nine squares on the snakes and ladders board, while being aware of the remaining two snakes, may be perceived as recovery (Kinchin 1998).

Errors of information processing

Scott and Palmer (2000) and others (on which the following is based) have highlighted errors of information processing in PTSD eases. Although there are now a significant number of books and papers on the subject of PTSD, and suggestions for diagnostic and treatment techniques, very few give any practical comments about recovery. Where PTSD is discussed, evidence is generally anecdotal and has been gleaned from the hundreds of PTSD survivors who have volunteered information as a way of supporting others and affirming their own identifiable milestones in recovery.

Occasionally, PTSD victims have encountered the following difficulties:

- ☹ Making unreasonable generalisations, e.g. All men are sexual abusers; Every teacher is a bully.
- ☹ Mentally filtering aspects of their trauma, e.g. seizing on a particularly gloomy aspect of an event and dwelling on it: 'He could have been killed doing that'.
- ☹ Believing 'all or nothing', e.g. everything is seen in the most extreme terms: 'I am either in control or I am not'.
- ☹ Labelling and 'mis-labelling' themselves, e.g. individuals focusing on their emotional state and drawing conclusions about themselves: 'Since it happened, I am frightened of my own shadow, I guess I am just a wimp'.
- ☹ A discounting attitude, e.g. disregarding any positive outcomes: 'I did my best, so what?'
- ☹ Magnification and minimisation of self-worth, e.g. magnification of shortcomings and making light of strengths: 'Since the trauma I am so irritable with my parents, and just about manage to keep going to school'.
- ☹ Making 'should' statements, inappropriate use of moral imperatives – *should* – *must* – *have* – *ought*, e.g. 'It's ridiculous that since the attack I now have to take my sister shopping with me. I *should* be able to do this by myself.'
- ☹ Jumping to conclusions, e.g. 'Everyone thinks I should be over this by now'.
- ☹ Over-personalisation of the situation; assuming that because something went wrong it must be the survivor's fault, e.g. 'I must have made a mistake somewhere for him to have died'.

Advice for those in early recovery

The following comments (after Aileen Quinton (1994) and others) are based upon personal experiences and although there is no research evidence to support them all, there is sufficient unresearched information to justify their inclusion here. There is a marked difference between the comments about survivors who have just set out on the road to recovery, and the comments describing those who have almost completed the journey and are in advanced stages of recovery.

Aileen Quinton, whose mother died in the Enniskillen bombing, suggests that a person suffering from PTSD should:

- ☺ Claim the right to experience and to express her own feelings.
- ☺ Allow herself to cry, since it can be very therapeutic.
- ☺ Take every opportunity to talk if this is helpful.
- ☺ Remember that it is the situation that is abnormal, not the trauma which is felt.
- ☺ Make contact with others in a similar situation, in order to feel relieved at how similar other victims feelings may be (the trauma bond).
- ☺ Be encouraged to progress in an individual way and at her own pace, taking 'breathing spaces' after achieving goals or accepting temporary regression of progress if necessary.
- ☺ Be prevented from 'pushing herself' too quickly in an attempt to please others.
- ☺ Being empowered to make her own decisions.

Revised thinking by PTSD survivors in advanced recovery

(The following is based on Quinton, Kinchin and others.)

Recovery is very difficult to assess. There are tests which provide a 'score' indicating the depth of traumatic experience. Therefore, if a test is administered and the survivor achieves a 'low score' it may be assumed a survivor is no longer traumatised and has recovered.

However, recovery is more a state of mind than it is a score in any psychoanalytical test. Recovery is a sense of achievement when something previously considered impossible is achievable and the victim feels it is well within grasp.

Recovery might include a person being able to think:

☺ I'm not so hard on myself these days.
☺ Things can be divided up into what really matters, and what doesn't really matter.
☺ I catch myself refocusing on the present.
☺ I can share with others.
☺ I have learned to cherish laughter.
☺ The pain of what happened has immunised me against most petty hurts.
☺ I focus on the present and the near future. I leave the past in the past.
☺ I am stronger because of what happened to me.
☺ I can use what happened to me to support others.
☺ Life has new meaning for me.
☺ I am starting to get bored with my story about the attack.
☺ My memories do not go away, but they are losing their gripping quality.
☺ My memories are no longer able to stop me in my tracks. I have control over them.
☺ I have the choice now; I can choose to leave it (the traumatic memory) if I want to.
☺ I can bear the pain of what happened.

Recovery from PTSD is very much akin to recovery from grief (Worden 1991). It is possible and indeed normal for a person to reach a healthy resolution to their grief. But the memory of the deceased person is still very real. Likewise, the memory of the trauma will remain for the PTSD victim. There will still be some remaining scar tissue. A child survivor of trauma may well have suffered academically and will have some catching-up to do if he wishes to regain his previous status with his peer group. This catching-up with academic work may be a realistic hurdle rather than an attempt to control the traumatic memory. Conversely, the fact that a child is still two reading books behind his classmates, or is some way behind with her mathematics project work, may serve as a reminder of the trauma and the consequences of being traumatised. Consequently, periods of depression, or even relapses into a state of traumatisation may result. If psychoanalytical tests which relate to PTSD are administered they may show a survivor as recovered, then as being traumatised, then achieving a score which shows recovery again. In the same way that a bereaved person may re-experience feelings of grief at anniversaries or other special moments, so a traumatised person may endure a brief re-experienceing of some traumatic symptoms.

Summary

When supporting children and adolescents (or adults) the authors believe that the snakes and ladders model is an approach which can be applied to all individuals because:

- it allows for the oscillations in recovery described by Horowitz (1979);
- it is easy to comprehend since almost everyone has some knowledge of the snakes and ladders game;
- the process of recovery is easily explained;
- although the snakes and ladders model appears to be very simple the model also demonstrates the complexity of PTSD, allowing for extremes of the disorder.

CHAPTER 9

Managing trauma in school

In recent years there have been several disasters and tragedies that have affected schools and pupils. At a time when schools are increasingly under pressure to ensure the academic performance of their pupils, the pastoral care of children may not appear to be a priority. An attitude seems to prevail which assumes tragedies and disasters happen to other people. There is of course a sense of security in this thought, but if schools are to fulfil their pastoral responsibilities and increase their effectiveness, they also need to be proactive in the development of strategic plans for crisis situations. This will enable them to respond to traumatic events and disasters quickly and effectively.

There are several reasons why schools should be the catalyst for this approach and not rely solely on support services and outside agencies:

- school staff know the members of the school community;
- school staff have expertise in meeting the individual needs of pupils;
- school staff are familiar with school organisation and routines;
- school staff are more likely to respect the privacy of adults and children.

A school case study

The head teacher of a small primary school returned after the weekend to be told two of the pupils in the reception class had fallen through the ice on the village pond and drowned. The dead children's brothers and sisters were also pupils at the school and they had witnessed the tragedy. One of the children's parents who was a secretary at the school had heard the children's screams for help and had called the emergency services. The families of the disaster victims, the school secretary, and indeed the whole school community looked to the head teacher for support and guidance.

What professional skills did the head teacher require?

- Skills of leadership and support within her school.
- Counselling skills.
- The capacity to coordinate support from outside agencies.
- Skills in crisis management.

What were the head teacher's personal needs?

- The capacity to deal with her own responses.

- Personal and professional support from staff and a support network outside the school in the short term and the long term.

What were the needs of the school family?

- Opportunities to share emotions and concerns.
- Information on the likely responses of siblings and the peer group of the deceased children.
- Information about what had happened in order to establish facts.
- Practical help and guidance from outside agencies.

Suggested framework for management of a traumatic incident in school

Although the effects of traumatic events are unique to the communities in which they occur, there are some general principles described by authors such as Yule and Gold (1993), Brown (1999) and Dyregrov (1991) which schools may find helpful.

Within the context of the framework offered, in this chapter 'traumatic experience' takes into account the effects on pupils, their families and staff of:

- the sudden death of someone known to them;
- the involvement of pupils or staff in an accident whilst out of school, e.g. traffic accident; fire; drowning;
- an incident in school such as a shooting; fire or physical attack;
- the effects of social violence.

It may also be helpful to differentiate between crisis and emergency. According to Hoff (1984), emergency differs from crisis. The former is the combination of unforeseen circumstances that call for immediate action (often with life and death implications), as opposed to crisis when a person develops a severe incapacity to cope, which is manifested as stress. Thus, stress is a symptom of crisis and crisis management is the process of working through the crisis.

The strategic plan – first steps

Children react to trauma in a variety of ways. It is a wisely held assumption (Stevenson 1994) that the most effective way of helping people cope is to prepare in advance of an actual event, since after the onset of a trauma there may be a period of 'psychic annulment' when people have difficulty assimilating information. In the immediate aftermath of a crisis people do not have the luxury of time for reflection and evaluation in a calm and thoughtful manner.

Many schools that have had firsthand experience of traumatic events have reflected on their response to what happened and developed a strategic plan for the future. It is important that all staff are involved so that they are familiar with the framework and they own it as the school policy. No plan can prevent the pain of trauma or the impact of the crisis. Neither is it possible to develop protocols for every crisis that might occur. However a framework that acknowledges the needs of individuals and the communities to which they belong may help to facilitate:

- opportunities to seek help;
- opportunities for people to regain control over their lives;
- opportunities to identify and cope with emotional responses.

Deciding on the rationale

The rationale will determine the way in which individual schools respond. The objectives should take into account the ethos of the school as it is written in the school prospectus. It is important all persons involved:

- share the purpose of the strategic plan;
- contribute towards the development of the strategic plan;
- have a supportive forum in which to share their views and concerns;
- are familiar with human response to loss, change and grief in both adults and children;
- are aware of the religious and cultural backgrounds of the families represented in the school.

Deciding who coordinates the work

It is suggested a member of the school management team coordinates the development of the strategic plan. The following people should be actively involved:

- the head teacher and all members of teaching and non-teaching staff;
- the school governors;
- parent representatives;
- community and faith group representatives.

Initial planning

There are a number of publications that suggest strategies for coping with crises in schools. Perhaps the best known of these is the book *Wise Before the Event: coping with crises in schools* by Yule and Gold (1993) and published by the Calouste Gulbenkian Foundation. The person with responsibility for coordinating the strategic plan should make themselves familiar with this publication and particularly the types of events which might occur in a school. Any events that are not listed but have already been experienced by the school should also be noted.

Ideally, the coordinator should have attended in-service training concerning the effects of trauma on children.

Drafting the strategic plan

A period of consultation will be necessary so that everyone involved feels their views have been taken into account. It is important to keep an educational perspective while also considering the rights and views of other persons such as parents and community members.

FIRST PRIORITY	• Obtain factual information at start of crisis	within hours
	• Senior management meet with school staff	within hours
	• Intervention team established	within hours
	• Contact families (as appropriate)	within hours
SECONDARY PRIORITY	• Call a staff meeting to give information	same day if practicable
	• Deal with the media	same day if practicable
	• Inform pupils in small groups (as appropriate)	same day if practicable
	• Call a debriefing meeting of staff involved in the crisis/disaster (as appropriate)	same day if practicable
	• Debrief pupils involved in crisis/disaster (as appropriate)	as soon as possible
	• Identify high risk pupils and staff	as soon as possible
	• Adjust to normal routines	as soon as possible
ONGOING TASKS	• Promote discussion in pupil groups	next few days and weeks
	• Identify need for individual/group counselling or other help	next days/weeks
	• Organise any counselling/support	as required

Figure 9.1 Managing a critical incident in school (based on Yule and Gold 1993, Brown 1999)

Dissemination of the strategic plan

Once the document is agreed, it should be circulated to all staff in the school. It is recommended it is easily accessible so that it can be referred to if an incident occurs

Responsibilities apportioned and training given

Yule and Gold (1993) suggest members of staff should be allocated responsibilities. The chart 'Managing a critical incident in school' (Figure 9.1) is based on the model used by Yule and Gold but has been divided according to management priorities.

Review and continuing development

The following should be taken into account:

- naming the person responsible for the review;
- the time scale between reviews;
- the format of the review;
- how the content and purpose will be shared with new staff;
- any government or local guidance.

First priorities in following the framework

- obtain factual information;
- senior management meet with school staff;
- establishing links with critical incident debriefing team;
- contact families (as appropriate).

Obtaining factual information

After a major incident it may be very difficult to establish accurate details of what has happened, particularly if the event occurred outside the school community. Establishing facts is very important because rumours can exacerbate distress. Communication between the school and any staff who are with children off site is a priority. Therefore schools should consider having more than one telephone line so that one may be designated as an emergency communication link if the need arises. Where this is not possible, a mobile telephone may be useful. Remember that reception may be poor.

Senior management meet with school staff

As soon as an incident has been confirmed, senior management should meet to establish as much factual information as possible so this can be shared with the remainder of the school staff. It is preferable to bring all personnel together, but whether this is possible or not will depend on the size of the school and the availability of staff.

Senior management responsibilities

Senior management should take responsibility for:

- dealing with telephone enquiries from parents or relatives; giving them emergency contact numbers where necessary, e.g. hospital, emergency disaster number;
- contacting the parents of children involved in the incident and advising them how further information will be conveyed;
- dealing with enquiries from the media.

Intervention team established

Senior management should establish an intervention team to activate agreed strategies. These will include:

- meeting parents who come to the school seeking more information and staying with them;
- arranging transport for parents who need to get to school;
- persons who will maintain normal routines as far as possible and make sure the welfare of pupils in the school is given priority;
- persons to liaise with others who have heard about the incident and come to the school.

Contact families and reunite children with parents

Children who have witnessed the event or been involved in the incident should be reunited with their families as soon as possible after any emergency intervention has taken place by medical or rescue services. Whether parents can be taken to the scene of the event will depend on how accessible it is to the school. If it is impossible to reunite families, senior management should do everything to establish telephone contact between young people and their parents.

Second priorities

- calling a staff meeting and giving information;
- dealing with the media;
- informing pupils in small groups (as appropriate);
- calling a debriefing meeting of staff involved in the crisis/disaster (as appropriate);
- debriefing pupils involved in the crisis/disaster (as appropriate);
- identifying high risk pupils and staff;
- adjusting to normal routines.

Calling a staff meeting and giving information

Where it has been possible to share information with all school staff soon after the event, it is important the initial information is updated and clarified at regular intervals. Where some staff do not know what has happened, senior management should call a meeting of all those who still need to be informed. No one on the staff should be excluded from this meeting since there will be tremendous pressure from parents, the local community and the media for information. Neither should the ongoing care and support of members of staff who have been the most affected by the incident fall to one or two senior managers in the school. In some cases it may be helpful to seek support from outside agencies, but generally, long-term support is best shared by members of the school community. Where outside support is sought, it should build on the efforts of the school staff and not seek to replace them. Where school staff have had professional development concerning the effects of loss, change and grief, the school community is more likely to be able to recognise its needs and to support individual persons.

Dealing with the media

When a traumatic event happens, it is likely the school will become the focus of attention. Schools have a pastoral responsibility to shield pupils and families from intrusion as much as possible. Therefore it is wise to appoint a senior member of staff who will take responsibility for the management of the media. Alternatively, the local education authority may provide personnel who will fulfil this role. Generally it is unwise to allow members of the press into the school.

Informing pupils

Children need clear, accurate information if they are to begin to make sense of what has happened. Where possible, class teachers or form tutors are probably the best people to break the news, since they know the pupils and will have established good communication with them in the past. This might be best done with smaller groups of pupils. Pupils should only be told information which is factual in order to prevent confusion and rumours. Written information should also be sent home to parents via their child. (See Figure 9.2 'Breaking sad news' later in this chapter.)

Calling a debriefing meeting

Many schools who have been involved in a traumatic event speak of the importance of bringing all those persons directly involved together as soon as possible after the incident. A debriefing meeting may help to:

- clarify what happened;
- reassure people that their feelings and responses are normal;
- identify people in need of specialist support from outside agencies.

Debriefing pupils

Adults will need to make themselves available to pupils who wish to talk about the event and children should be encouraged to do this although nobody should be forced to do so. After a few days have elapsed many pupils will welcome a return to normal school routines but they should feel secure in the knowledge that staff are still available to listen to their concerns in the days and weeks ahead.

Identifying high risk pupils and staff

Schools will find it useful to designate a member of staff to fulfil the role of a supportive-carer for pupils and adults. It is important to recognise each person involved in the traumatic event will have an individual response. Where schools have taken part in professional development that has made reference to Post-Traumatic Stress Disorders, they will be better equipped to recognise adults and children who may be at high risk. If children or adults have died, it is essential the school acknowledges this and extends sympathy to the families concerned. In most cases bereaved families will appreciate representatives from the school at funerals.

Adjusting to normal routines

In the immediate aftermath of a traumatic event it is essential to acknowledge what has happened and to give people opportunities to express their feelings and to reflect on the fact that life will never be the same again. But it is also important to establish normal routines so that pupils feel secure. Where children return to school soon afterwards, they may still be suffering from shock and trauma. The following may help:

- listening to worries and concerns;
- allowing part-time attendance at first;
- making arrangements for a quiet place either with or without an adult if this is desired;
- reassurance that extra support will be given if a child's academic performance has suffered;
- reassurance that help from outside the school can be sought if the child and their parents desire this;
- encouraging children to be patient in their reactions.

Ongoing tasks

These will include:

- promoting discussion in pupil groups, as appropriate;
- identifying need for individual/group counselling or other help;
- organising any counselling/support.

Promoting discussion in pupil groups

Although individual schools should adopt a policy which will support children from the time of the traumatic event and meet their individual needs, the following framework for promoting discussion in pupil groups may be helpful. The facilitator should have a sound knowledge of children's responses to loss, change and grief.

Stage 1 – Explaining the purpose of the meeting
The setting where children are introduced to discussion groups should be familiar to them and should be facilitated by their own teacher or form tutor where ever possible. Confidentiality should be established at the onset of the discussion and pupils should be reassured they may express their feelings in any way they wish as long as they are not hurting themselves or anyone else. Although all who are present are invited to participate in the meeting, there is no expectation that everyone will speak or contribute if they do not wish to do so.

Stage 2 – Children telling what they know about the event
At this stage pupils are encouraged to share with the adult what they know about the trauma. Therefore it is important this person has a thorough and accurate knowledge of what happened so that any misunderstandings or confusion can be clarified. Providing children with concrete information helps them to come to terms with what has happened and to allay any misconceptions or rumours.

Stage 3 – Describing feelings at the time of the event
Helping children to articulate the way they felt when they first heard about the event or witnessed what was happening, provides a bridge between the event and the emotional responses that have developed afterwards. It is important that where children are asked any questions these are open-ended, encouraging them to reveal as much or as little as they wish.

Stage 4 – Sharing feelings experienced between the event and the present time
When children are encouraged to share their feelings soon after the event, they are more likely to be able to identify their responses up to the present time. Because emotions may be difficult to describe and the intensity of the feelings may be very powerful, hearing how other people have responded may help individual children to feel less isolated and more in control. Putting thoughts into words can be very helpful, but some pupils may prefer to draw or to write about the event. Young children may 'play out' what happened.

Stage 5 – Collecting thoughts together and describing individual and group responses
At this stage, the role of the adult is to summarise what actually happened and to describe the thoughts and feelings that have been shared by the children. Reassurance should be given to individuals and to the group that their responses will vary and the intensity of emotions may be greater at some times than at others.

Stage 6 – Looking to the future
Because children may feel very vulnerable after a tragic event, it is important they are helped to feel safe and be given opportunities to plan what will happen in the time ahead. In the short term this may include attending funerals, deciding on memorials or some other way of marking what has happened.

Identifying the need for individual or group counselling or other help

Throughout the book we have learned that people who have been involved in a traumatic event will take time adjusting to what has happened. Generally those people whose lives were at greatest risk are likely to suffer the most stress and trauma. In addition, where victims have home circumstances that are unsettled or in the case of persons with special educational needs, the likelihood of Post-Traumatic Stress Disorders seems to be increased. Thoughts and memories of the event will often monopolise their thoughts. In children the effects of grief can lead to a lack of concentration, changed behaviour and a decline in their academic performance. Physical illnesses such as headaches, stomach upsets and joint pains may also occur. Where children are lacking information about how an event occurred, this may result in fantasies that can be extremely distressing.

Problems are particularly likely and prolonged where siblings or peers have been injured or killed and children have been unable to receive the support they have needed after the event (van Eerdewegh et al. 1985). In extreme cases children may lose confidence in their own future, because they feel vulnerable and fearful the event may reoccur (Dyregrov 1991). This is more likely where children witness social violence and warfare.

The developmental level of children seems to have a bearing on how their behaviour may be changed. Younger children may be less independent than they were before the event and they are more likely to regress in skills that have already been mastered. Likewise, older children often demonstrate behaviour that was characteristic of themselves at a younger age.

Some children will find great difficulty relating to their peer group and they may feel different and be prone to bullying or teasing. In addition, because friends may not know how to respond, they may avoid the child who is grieving which results in social isolation (Abrams 1992).

The way in which children experience a trauma or are told about it plays a large part in their reactions. Whatever the circumstances, they will need time to adjust and to work through both the event and their grief responses to the event. Dyregrov (1991) believes the problems that many children encounter in their grief are related to the circumstances of the event.

Responses to trauma

The responses to the trauma may be shown through:

- physical, emotional or developmental delay;
- fear of new situations;
- changed behaviour, e.g. hair-twisting, thumb-sucking, rocking;
- self injury;
- extremes of passivity or aggression;
- stealing;
- fantasies;
- incontinence;
- eating disorders;
- personality changes;
- pessimism about the future;
- poor self-esteem.

Many of the principles already discussed which relate to caring for bereaved children will be relevant to children recovering from a traumatic event. Some of the advantages of facilitating discussion between pupils in small groups have been outlined earlier in the chapter. Sometimes pupils will need additional support from outside the school that will encourage them to develop coping strategies. Schools do however have a responsibility towards families as well as towards the pupils in their care. It is essential the parents of pupils are consulted together with the young people themselves before help is sought from outside agencies. Furthermore, the reliability of support services and the experience and qualifications of individuals should be checked before they are invited to the school.

The parameters of the impact of crisis are not always limited to the school environment as the following illustrates.

A group of Year 9 pupils were on a field trip to the South West of England. While studying the ecology of the rock pools at low tide, a car plunged over the cliff directly behind them and the two people inside were hurled out of the vehicle on to the rocks.

The safety of the school children does not end the experience for the pupils, their teacher or their parents. The effects of the crisis impact on the school community and the thoughts of what might have been.

Essentially the role of support services should be to build on the caring role of the school and the skills possessed by the staff, rather than attempting to replace these. Yule and Gold (1993) describe what they call 'ground rules to observe when working with outside consultants'. These include:

- agreeing the boundaries of confidential information;
- clarifying personnel to be informed when concern is raised about a child;
- facilitating regular meetings between any support agencies and teaching staff.

Perhaps the most important strategy to adopt is to listen to what individual people say about what they want, rather than assuming a need. Empathy and compassion are human capacities but they are developed through practise more often than they are learned through the pages of textbooks.

Many support agencies will have people working for them who have expertise in helping people to adapt to loss, change and grief, but almost without exception people who are already known to individuals will provide better support than personnel who may imagine themselves to be the 'experts'.

Responding to sad events in school

From the early days of childhood most children form friendships and as they grow older relationships develop which may be extremely intense and long-lasting. When a peer dies children's grief is not unlike that associated with the death of a sibling. The death is seen to be unjust and untimely; hence it may trigger bitter feelings, coupled with a sense of loneliness and isolation. It is quite normal for children to reflect on how the situation might have been if it was themselves who had died. This happens especially if the death occurred in violent of tragic circumstances or if the place of death was one friends had frequented.

Each child is part of a school family in addition to belonging to their home. Therefore it is important if a child or someone known to the school community dies, people are able to express their sadness acknowledging the contribution that the person made to the community.

Parents need to know how a school has responded and what information has been given to their child. This will include:

- factual information about the circumstances of the illness or death;
- information about how their child may respond after hearing the news;
- suggestions for books that may help their child understand the event.

Rituals and ceremonies

Children need to participate in rituals and ceremonies since these events will give concrete expression to their thoughts and feelings. It also allows them to acknowledge what has happened and to confront the reality of their loss. But for ceremonies to be a helpful part of coming to terms with what has happened, children should be involved as much or as little as they wish. Adults need to have their views respected too, especially since there are a great variety of cultural and religious views concerning children and funeral rites. Parents should never be persuaded against their wishes to let a child go to a funeral. Neither should a child be forced to go. However, children who have had an opportunity to attend are generally glad they went. Those who were prevented may grow up to regret they were not given the choice.

How should schools respond to bereaved families?

It is important that schools

- maintain contact and express sympathy;
- be aware of cultural and religious beliefs or practices;
- encourage the family to maintain control over any decisions which need to be made;
- respect privacy where this is requested.

Breaking sad news to an individual child	Breaking sad news to groups of children
Who should tell the child? • Someone who is known and trusted by the child. • Someone who can maintain contact with the child in the time ahead. • Someone who has a sound knowledge of how children respond to trauma. • Someone who allows the child to express their feelings. **Where should the child be told?** • In a familiar place. • In safe and comfortable surroundings. • In a private place. **How should the news be given?** • In language which is easily understood. • In language which is factual. • With opportunities for the child to ask questions. • With opportunities for the child to show emotional responses. • With an opportunity for the adult to establish the child has understood the news which has been given.	**Who should tell the children?** • Someone who is known and trusted by the children. • Someone who is confident speaking to the group. • Someone who has a sound knowledge of how children respond to trauma. • Someone who respects children's confidentiality. **How should children be told?** • In a familiar setting, preferably a classroom, rather than a large hall. • In language which is easily understood by them. • By giving them factual information which is consistent with information which other children in the school are given. • With sufficient time available to answer questions and raise concerns.

Figure 9.2 Breaking sad news

If families conduct private funerals, schools may choose to hold a memorial service, where children are encouraged to take an active part in how they will say 'good-bye'. If the death occurred in traumatic circumstances, a ceremony may prove to be therapeutic, signifying that the event is over. Although people feel sad, the school community is able to plan for the future.

How might schools respond?

The following might be considered:

- suggest pupils and staff representatives who might attend the funeral;
- arrange a special assembly or an act of collective worship in school;
- arrange a memorial service in school and encourage pupils to contribute;
- light a candle which burns between the death and the funeral; provide a tangible memorial such as planting a tree or making a memory book; mark the anniversary of the death.

Summary

In recent years there have been a number of disasters and tragedies that have affected schools and pupils. Many of these schools have reflected on their response to what happened and they have developed a strategic plan for the future. Others hope a critical incident will not occur. There is of course a sense of security in this thought but if schools are to fulfil their pastoral responsibilities, they need to be proactive in the development of strategic plans for crisis situations.

No plan can prevent the pain of the trauma or the impact of the crisis. However a framework that acknowledges the needs of individuals and the community to which they belong may help to facilitate:

- opportunities to seek support;
- opportunities for people to regain control over their lives;
- opportunities to identify and cope with emotional responses.

Everyone affected by a critical event will take time to adjust to what happened and to work through their grief responses. Many of the principles that relate to caring for bereaved people and are discussed elsewhere in the book will be relevant to crisis management. Perhaps the most important strategy to develop is for adults to listen to what individual pupils are able to communicate about their needs.

References

Abrams, R. (1992) *When Parents Die*. London: Letts.

Aldgate, J. and Simmonds, J. (eds) (1988) *Work with Children*. London: British Agencies for Adoption and Fostering.

American Psychiatric Association (1952) *Diagnostic & Statistical Manual of Mental Disorders (DSM)*. Washington DC: American Pyschiatric Association.

American Psychiatric Association (1968) *Diagnostic & Statistical Manual of Mental Disorders (DSM II)*. Washington DC: American Pyschiatric Association.

American Psychiatric Association (1980) *Diagnostic & Statistical Manual of Mental Disorders (DSM III)*. Washington DC: American Pyschiatric Association.

American Psychiatric Association (1987) *Diagnostic & Statistical Manual of Mental Disorders (DSM III R)*. Washington DC: American Pyschiatric Association.

American Psychiatric Association (1994) *Diagnostic & Statistical Manual of Mental Disorders (DSM IV)*. Washington DC: American Pyschiatric Association.

Armstrong-Dailey, A. (1995) 'Care of the dying child', in Grollman, E. (ed.) *Bereaved Children and Teens – A support guide for parents and professionals*. Boston: Bacon Press.

Austin, T. (1967) *Aberfan: The story of a disaster*. London: Hutchinson.

Bacon, D. (1994) 'Spiritual and cultural aspects', in Goldman, A. (ed.) *Care of the Dying Child*. Oxford: Oxford University Press.

Bergen, M. (1958) 'Effect of severe trauma on a 4-year old child', *Psychoanalytic Study of the Child* 13, 407–29.

Black, D. (1989) 'Life threatening illness, children and family therapy', *Journal of Family Therapy* 22, 18–24.

Black, D. and Urbanowicz, M. A. (1987) 'Family intervention with bereaved children', *Journal of Child Psychology and Psychiatry* 28, 467–76.

Bluebond-Langner, M. (1978) *The Private Worlds of Dying Children*. New York: Wiley.

Bluebond-Langner, M. (1995) 'Worlds of dying children and their well siblings', in Doka, K. (ed.) *Children Mourning, Mourning Children*. Washington: Hospice Association of America.

Blumenthal, S. (1988) 'Suicide: a guide to risk factors, assessment and treatment of suicidal patients', *Medical Clinics of North America* 72(4), 937–71.

Breslau, N. (1982) 'Siblings of disabled children: birth order and age-spacing effects', *Journal of Abnormal Child Psychology* 10, 85–96.

Brown, E. (1994) 'Children, death and grief', unpublished MA dissertation, Oxford.

Brown, E. (1999) *Loss, Change and Grief: An educational perspective*. London: David Fulton Publishers.

Brown, G. and Harris, T. (1989) *Social Origins of Depression*. London: Tavistock.

Bugen, L. (ed.) (1979) 'Human grief: a model for prediction and intervention', in Bugen, L. (ed.) *Death and Dying: Theory, Research, Practice*. Idaho: William Brown.

Burke, J. *et al.* (1982) 'Changes in children's behaviour after a natural disaster', *American Journal of Psychiatry* 139, 1010–14.

Calouste Gulbenkian Foundation (1995) *Children and Violence*. London: Calouste Gulbenkian Foundation.

Cattermole, F. (1990) 'Foreword', in Garrett, B. *Spiritual Development of Young People* Briefings No. 10. London: National Council for Voluntary Youth Services.

Children Act (1989) *A Guide for the Education Service*. Milton Keynes: Open University Press.

Cleaver, H. and Freeman, M. (1995) *Parental Perspectives in Cases of Suspected Child Abuse*. London: HMSO.

Cohen, D. (1991) *Aftershock: The psychological and political consequences of disaster*. London: Paladin.

Compton, M. (1998) *Children, Spirituality, Religion and Social Work*. Aldershot: Ashgate.

Creighton, S. J. (1992) *Child Abuse Trends in England and Wales 1988–1990, And an overview from 1973–1990*. London: NSPCC.

Culling, J. A. (1988) 'The psychological problems of families and children', in Oakhill, A. (ed.) *The Supportive Care of the Child with Cancer*. Bristol: John Wright.

Deblinger, E., Lippmann, J. and Steer, R. (1996) 'Sexually abused children suffering post traumatic stress symptoms: initial treatment findings', *Child Maltreatment* 1(4), 310–21.

Department of Health (1991) *Working Together Under the Children Act 1989: A guide to arrangements for inter-agency co-operation for the protection of children from abuse*. London: HMSO.

Doka, K. (ed.) (1993) *Children Mourning, Mourning Children*. Washington: Hospice Association of America.

Draijer, N. (1994) 'Major developments in research in the long-term sequelea of child sexual abuse', Paper at International Conference 'Violence in the Family', Amsterdam, Netherlands.

Dwivedi, K. N. (ed.) (2000) *Post-Traumatic Stress Disorder in Children and Adolescents*. London: Whurr Publishers.

Dyregrov, A. (1991) *Grief in Children – A Handbook for Adults*. London: Jessica Kingsley.

Eiser, C. (1993) *Growing Up with a Childhood Disease – The impact on children and their families*. London: Jessica Kingsley.

Eiser, C. and Havermans, T. (1994) 'Treatment of childhood cancer and implications for long-term social adjustment: a review', *Archives of Disease in Childhood* 70, 66–70.

Erikson, K. T. (1976) *Everything in its Path: Destruction of Community in Buffalo Creek Flood*. New York: Simon & Schuster.

Fahlberg, V. (1984) *A Child's Journey Through Placement*. London: British Agencies for Adoption and Fostering.

Fahrenback, P. *et al.* (1986) 'Adolescent sexual offenders, offenders and offence characteristics', *American Journal of Orthopsychiatry* 56, 2.

Furness, T. (1991) *The Multi Professional Handbook of Child Sexual Abuse*. London: Routledge.

Garmezy, N. and Rutter, M. (1985) 'Acute reactions to stress', in Rutter, M. and Hersov, L. (eds) *Child and Adolescent Psychiatry: Modern approaches*, 2nd edn. Oxford: Blackwell.

Godden, R. (1989) *A House with Four Rooms – Autobiography*, vol. 2. London: Macmillan.

Gordon, L. (1989) *Heroes of their Own Lives: A Study of 120 Years of Sexual Abuse in America*. London: Virago.

Green, B. L. *et al.* (1991) 'Children and disaster: age, gender and parental effects on PTSD symptoms', *Journal of the American Academy of Child and Adolescent Psychiatry* 30, 945–51.

Hamblen, J. (1998) 'PTSD in Children and Adolescents' http://www.ncptsd.org/facts/

Hambling, J. (1997) 'On the Efficacy of CISD' http://www.ozemail.com.au/

Herbert, M. (1991) *Clinical Child Psychology: Social Learning, Behaviour and Development*. Chichester: Wiley.

Herbert, M. (1996) *Supporting Bereavement and Dying Children and their Parents*. Leicester: The British Psychological Society.

Hobfoll, S. (1991) 'Gender differences in stress reactions: women filling the gaps', *Psychology and Health* 5, 95–110.

Hodgkinson, P. and Stewart, M. (1991) *Coping with Catastrophe – A Handbook of Disaster Management*. London: Routledge.

Hoff, L. A. (1984) *People in Crisis*. California: Addison Wesley.

Horowitz, M. (1978) *Stress Response Syndromes*, New York: Aronson.

Horowitz, M. J. (1979) 'Psychological response to serious life events', in Hamilton, V. and Warburton, D. (eds) *Human Stress and Cognition: An information processing approach*. New York: Wiley.

James, L., Titchener, M. D. and Kapp, F. C. (1976) 'Family and character change at Buffalo Creek', *American Journal of Psychiatry* 133(3), 295–99.

Judd, D. (1989) *Give Sorrow Words – Working with a dying child*. London: Free Association Books.

Kastenbaum, R. (1969) 'Death and bereavement in later life', in Kutscher, A. (ed.) *Death and Bereavement*. Illinois: Charles Thomas.

Kastenbaum, R. (1997) *Death, Society and Human Experience*, 2nd edn. St Louis: Mosby.

Kennedy, M. (1995) 'Perceptions of abused disabled children', in Wilson, K. and James, A. (eds) *The Child Protection Handbook*. London: Tindall.

Kinchin, D. (1988) 'Fatal RTA: child involved', *Police Review* 1 July, 1380–81.

Kinchin, D. (1992) 'Telophobia', *Nursing Times* 88(52), 28–29.

Kinchin, D. (1994) *Post Traumatic Stress Disorder: A practical guide to recovery*. London: HarperCollins.

Kinchin, D. (1997) 'Post Traumatic Stress Disorder: Aromatherapy and physiotherapy can be a prelude to effective counselling', *Alternative Therapies in Clinical Practice* 4(2), 55–56.

Kinchin, D. (1998) *Post Traumatic Stress Disorder: The invisible injury*. Oxon: Success Unlimited.

Knudson, A. G. and Natterson, J. M. (1960) 'Participation of parents in the hospital care of their fatally ill children', *Pediatrics* 26, 482–90.

Kroth, J. A. (1988) 'Family Therapy impact on intrafamilial child sexual abuse', Paper at Second International Congress of Child Abuse and Neglect, London.

Kupst, M. J. (1992) 'Long term family coping with acute lymphoblastic leukaemia', in LaGreca, A. M. *et al.* (eds) *Stress and Coping in Child Health*. New York: Guildford Press.

Lacey, G. (1972) 'Observations on Aberfan', *Journal of Psychosomatic Research* 16, 257–60.

Lansdown, R. and Goldman, A. (1988) 'The psychological care of children with malignant disease', *Journal of Child Psychology and Psychiatry* 29(5), 555–67.

Lifton, R. J. (1983) 'Responses of survivors to man-made catastrophes', *Bereavement Care* 2, 2–6.

Lonigan, C., *et al.* (1991) 'Children's reactions to a natural disaster: symptom severity and degree of exposure', *Advances in Behaviour Research and Therapy* 13, 135–54.

Mallon, B. (1997) *Helping Children to Manage Loss: Positive Strategies for Renewal and Growth.* London: Jessica Kingsley.

Marr, N. and Field, T. (2001) *Bullycide: Death at playtime.* Oxon: Success Unlimited.

Massey, R. K. (1985) 'The constant shadow: reflections on the life of a chronically ill child', in Hobbs, N. and Perrin, J. (eds) *Issues in the Care of Children with Chronic Disease.* San Francisco: Jossey Bass.

Mayou, R., Bryant, B. and Duthie, R. (1993) 'Psychiatric consequences of road traffic accidents', *British Medical Journal* 307, 647–51.

McFarlane, A. C. and Blumbergs, V. (1985) 'The relationship between psychiatric impairment and natural disaster: the role of distress', Department of Psychiatry, The Flinders University of South Australia, unpublished paper.

McGoldrick, M. (1982) 'Ethnicity and family therapy', in McGoldrick, M., Pearce, J. K. and Giardano, J. (eds) *Ethnicity and Family Therapy.* New York: Guildford Press.

Miller, J. (1974) *Aberfan: A disaster and its aftermath.* London: Constable.

Moody, R. and Moody, C. (1991) 'A family perspective – helping children acknowledge and express grief following death', *Death Studies* 15, 587–602.

Nagy, S. and Ungerer, J. (1990) 'The adaption of mothers and fathers to children with cystic fibrosis: a comparison', *Children's Health Care* 19, 147–54.

Narayanasamy, A. (1993) 'Nurses' awareness and preparation in meeting their patients' spiritual needs', *Nurse Education Today* 13, 196–201.

National Children's Home (1992) *Annual Report.*

NCH Action for Children (1994) *The Hidden Victims: Children and Domestic Violence.* London: NCH Action for Children.

NCH Action for Children (1995) *Fact file '95.* London: NCH Action for Children.

NSPCC (1995) *Survey of Childhood Experiences: Sexual abuse: summary.* London: NSPCC.

Osborn, A. (2000) 'Gunman shot as hostage crisis ends' *Guardian,* 2 June.

Pandit, S. and Shah, L. (2000) 'Post-traumatic stress disorder: causes and aetiological factors', in Dwivedi, K. (ed.) *Post-traumatic Stress Disorder in Children and Adolescents.* London: Whurr.

Parker, J., Watts, H. and Allsopp, M. R. (1995) 'Post-traumatic stress symptoms in children and parents following a school-based fatality', *Child Care Health and Development* 21(3), 183–89.

Parkes, C. M. (1983) *Recovery from Bereavement.* New York: Basic Books.

Pfeffer, C. (1986) *The Suicidal Child.* New York: Guildford Press.

Phillimore, P., Beattie, A. and Townsend, P. (1994) 'Widening inequality in Northern England (1981–1991), *British Medical Journal* 308, (6937), 1125–28.

Puffer, M. K., Greenwald, R. and Elrod, D. E. (1998) 'A single session EMDR study with 20 traumatised children and adolescents', Traumatology e 3:2 art 6. http://www.fsu.edu/~trauma/

Pynoos, R. (1992) 'Grief and trauma in children and adolescents', *Bereavement Care* 11(1), 2–10.

Pynoos, R. *et al.* (1987) 'Life threat and post traumatic stress in school-age children', *Archives of General Psychiatry* 44, 1057–63.

Pynoos, R. and Nader, L. (1998) 'Psychological first aid and treatment approach to children exposed to community violence: research implications', *Journal of Traumatic Stress* 1, 444–73.

Quinton, A. (1994) Unpublished lecture notes.

Randall, P., and Parker, J. (1997) 'Traumatic stress disorder and children of school age', *Educational Psychology in Practice* 13(3), 197–203.

Rando, T. A. (1993) 'Creating therapeutic rituals in the psychotherapy of the bereaved', *Psychotherapy* 22, 236–40.

Raphael, B. (1984) *The Anatomy of Bereavement. A Handbook for the Caring Professions.* London: Hutchinson.

Raphael, B. (1986) *When Disaster Strikes: A handbook for the caring professionals.* London: Unwin Hyman.

Redmond, L. (1989) *Surviving: When someone you love was murdered.* Florida: Psychological Consultation and Education Service.

Ritter, S. (1989) *Bethlem Royal and Maudsley Hospital Manual of Clinical Psychiatric Nursing Principles and Procedures.* London: Harper and Collins.

Robinson, R. C. and Mitchell, J. T. (1993) 'Evaluation of psychological debriefings', *Journal of Traumatic Stress* 6(3), 367–82.

Rose, S. (2000) 'Evidence based practice will affect the way we work', *Counselling* 12(2), 105–07.

Rynearson, E. (1987) 'Psychological adjustment to unnatural dying', in Zisook, S. (ed.) *Biopsychosocial Aspects of Bereavement.* Washington: American Psychiatric Press.

Saylor, C. F. (ed.) (1993) *Children and Disaster.* New York: Plenum Press.

Schofield, G. (1997) 'Protection and loss: the impact of separation on the abused and neglected child', in Lindsay, B. and Elsegood, J. (eds) *Working with Children in Grief and Loss.* London: Bailliere Tindall.

Scott, M. J. and Palmer, S. (2000) *Trauma and Post-traumatic Stress Disorder.* London: Cassell.

Smith, J. (1986) 'Sealing over and integration: models of resolution in the post-traumatic stress recovery process', in Figley, C. R. (ed.) *Trauma and its Wake,* vol. 2. New York: Brunner Mazel.

Spinetta, J. (1984) 'Measurement of family function, communication and cultural effects', *Cancer* 53, 2230–37.

Stephenson, J. (1985) *Death, Grief and Mourning.* New York: The Free Press.

Stern, G. M. (1976) *The Buffalo Creek Disaster.* New York: Vintage Books.

Stevenson, R. (ed.) (1994) *What Can we Do? Preparing a School Community to Cope with Crisis.* New York: Baywood.

Stoll, R. (1989) 'The essense of spirituality', in Carson, V. B. (ed.) *Spiritual Dimensions of Nursing Practice.* Philadelphia: Saunders.

Terr, L. C. (1981) 'Psychic trauma in children: observations following the Chowchilla school-bus kidnapping', *American Journal of Psychiatry* 138(1), 14–19.

Terr, L. C. (1983) 'Chowchilla revisited: the effects of psychic trauma four years after a school-bus kidnapping', *American Journal of Psychiatry* 140(12), 1543–50.

Thoburn, J., Lewis, A. and Shemmings, D. (1995) *Paternalism or Partnership? Family Involvement in the Child Protection Process.* London: HMSO.

Tsui, E. (1991) 'The "Jupiter" sinking disaster: effects on teenagers' school performance', unpublished MSc dissertation, University of London.

Tylor, E. (1871) *Primitive Culture.* London: John Murray.

Udwin, O. (1993) 'Children's reactions to traumatic events', *Journal of Child Psychology and Psychiatry* 34(2), 115–27.

UNICEF (1995) *The Convention on the Rights of the Child* (Information Kit). London: UNICEF.

Valente, S., Saunders, J. and Street, R. (1988) 'Adolescent bereavement following suicide: an examination of relevant literature', *Journal of Counselling and Development* 67, 174–77.

Van Eerdewegh, M. *et al.* (1985) 'The bereaved child', *British Journal of Psychiatry* 140, 23–29.

Vandvick, I. H. and Eckblad, G. (1991) 'Mothers of children with recent onset of rheumatic disease: Associations between maternal distress, psychosocial variables and the disease of the children', *Developmental and Behavioural Pediatrics* 12, 84–91.

Waechter, E. (1971) 'Death anxiety in children with fatal illness', unpublished thesis, Washington..

Wass, H. and Stillion, J. (1988) 'Death in the lives of children and adolescents', in Wass, H., Berardo, F. and Neimeyer, R. (eds) *Dying: Facing the Facts.* Washington: Hemisphere.

Williams, T. (1993) 'Trauma in the workplace', in Wilson, J. P. and Raphael, B. (eds) *International Handbook of Traumatic Stress.* New York: Plenum Press

Worden, J. W. (1991) *Grief Counselling and Grief Therapy.* London: Routledge.

Yule, W. (1999) *Post-Traumatic Stress Disorder: Concepts and theory.* Chichester: Wiley.

Yule, W. and Canterbury, R. (1994) 'The treatment of post traumatic stress disorder in children and adolescents', *International Review of Psychiatry* 6, 141–51.

Yule, W. and Gold, A. (1993) *Wise Before the Event: Coping with crises in schools.* London: Calouste Gulbenkian Foundation.

Yule, W. and Udwin, O. (1991) 'Screening child survivors for post-traumatic stress disorders: experiences from the "Jupiter" sinking', *British Journal of Clinical Psychology* 30, 131–38.

Yule, W. and Williams, R. M. (1990) 'Post-traumatic stress reactions in children', *Journal of Traumatic Stress* 3(3), 279–95.

Index